Professional **Development** for *Successful* Classrooms

Teaching Social Studies Today

Sara Shoob, M.Ed., and
Cynthia Stout, Ph.D.

SHELL EDUCATION

Teaching Social Studies Today

Editor
Wendy Conklin, M.A.

Assistant Editor
Torrey Maloof

Editorial Director
Emily R. Smith, M.A.Ed.

Editor-in-Chief
Sharon Coan, M.S.Ed.

Editorial Manager
Gisela Lee, M.A.

Creative Director
Lee Aucoin

Cover Designer
Lesley Palmer

Print Production
Juan Chavolla

Publisher
Corinne Burton, M.A.Ed.

Shell Education

5301 Oceanus Drive

Huntington Beach, CA 92649

http://www.shelleducation.com

ISBN 978-1-4258-0171-7

© 2008 Shell Educational Publishing, Inc.
Reprinted 2010

Table of Contents

Table of Contents *(cont.)*

Table of Contents *(cont.)*

Table of Contents *(cont.)*

Introduction

The intended audience for this book is the novice teacher. The authors hope that this book will start teachers on their journey across the bridge of practice and experience to the other side; that of master teacher. However, the topics discussed will not only benefit the teacher new to the profession, but also the teacher who desires to continue the search for up-to-date research and practical applications.

Many who teach social studies are acutely aware and concerned about the place of the social sciences in today's classroom. Legislation on the national level (No Child Left Behind) and state and local levels (standards, proficiencies, and state tests) are emphasizing reading, writing, and mathematics to the exclusion of the social sciences and science. This is particularly critical at the elementary level and, in some cases, middle school as well. Sadly, some schools have a few weeks of social studies and then the content changes to a few weeks of science. Another major objective of this book is to illustrate (through example) the innumerable ways the skills and content of the social sciences connect to and enhance the learning of other disciplines. More importantly, however, is to demonstrate the importance of the social sciences to students' lives as they leave our classrooms and become the citizens of tomorrow.

A third and final reason for this book is to solidify teacher learning as he or she progresses through this book. Gone are the days of reading the chapter, answering the comprehension questions, and then taking the test. The authors have deliberately included "tasks" for teachers reading this text that serve two purposes: to provide the opportunity for self-reflection, which results in more effective learning, and in doing so, to model strategies or structures teachers can use with their own students for the same purpose.

How This Book Is Organized

This book is organized with chapters on specific topics designed to take readers through a process which effective teachers use in their daily practice. Within each chapter are examples of strategies at primary, elementary, and secondary levels. At the end of each chapter, teachers will have the opportunity to reflect on their practices and create plans for how they might implement the discussed topic in their classrooms. It is the authors' hope that teachers will revisit these reflections over the course of a year or so and note the changes they have discovered in their teaching.

As teachers embark upon this journey, they will want to keep several things in mind. First, they should engage their students in the pedagogy/strategies/lenses of the social sciences (civics, economics, geography, and history). Thus, what does a "historian" (political scientist, economist, geographer) do? What are the thought processes in which the "historian" engages? How are they like those in the other disciplines? How do they differ? What tools do those in each discipline use? How might those tools be used to enhance the work of the practitioner? For example, what purpose do maps serve for the historian? How do charts and graphs help both the economist and the geographer illustrate data?

Second, teachers should remember that techniques need to be revisited, re-taught, and practiced many times by students to insure their mastery of skills germane to the study of the social sciences. Teachers need to be fully aware of the levels of the students in their classrooms and adapt those techniques for a variety of learning levels. Remember, the same technique can be used K–12 if students are asked to become more independent in its use with each grade level. What resources can be used with lower level readers? How can this technique be deepened for the gifted students in the classroom? What does a particular technique look like in the upper elementary grades? How does the same technique change with middle school students?

Finally, teachers should carefully choose strategies with these critical questions in mind:

- Why am I having my students learn this?
- What do I want them to know and be able to do?
- How will I know my students are successful?
- What actions will I take if they are not?

With that, teachers are ready to begin their journey. Travel safely and enjoy!

Vocabulary Review

Education is notorious for its jargon. Many of the terms specific to the topic of social studies are used in this book. In order to have a better understanding of these particular terms, complete the vocabulary review below. Before reading on in the book, note your initial definition in the first column. Then, when you have finished reading the book, note your final definition of each term, and see whether your definitions have changed. You will also find the definition of each of these terms in the Glossary (pages 189–192).

Term	My First Definition	My Final Definition
assessment		
auditory learner		
authentic tasks		
Bloom's taxonomy		
case studies		
concepts		
constructed response		

Term	My First Definition	My Final Definition
constructivist learning		
cooperative learning		
diagnostic assessment		
expository text		
formative assessment		
graphic organizer		
integration		
learning style		
modeling		
performance-based assessment		
primary source		

Term	My First Definition	My Final Definition
prior knowledge		
problem-based learning		
rubric		
secondary source		
social studies		
summarizing		
summative assessment		
tactile/kinesthetic learner		
visual learner		

Creating the Social Studies Classroom

Why Teach Social Studies?

As social studies teachers begin to think about their answers to this question and their rationale for what they do and believe in passionately, their first responses tend to be skill oriented: critical thinking, preparing students to be good citizens, encourage lifelong learning, etc. Then, there is a "light-bulb" moment when the teacher realizes the critical nature of what he or she does. What content area explains us as human beings, connects us to our world physically and culturally, tells us where we have been and helps us understand where we are going and why, and explains the reasons for the choices we make and the ways we organize our lives? The answer, of course, is social studies. It is not over-stating the case to acknowledge that a solid grounding in the social sciences results in a better understanding of the other disciplines. Certainly, social studies teachers view their discipline as the center of a solid education.

Given the vital importance of all that social studies teachers teach and the waning time in which students have to learn the lessons, thorough planning and "working smart" are imperative. Part of working smart is providing students with a learning environment that promotes constructivist learning, where the student is the center and the teacher works as "the guide on the side." So, what does that learning environment look like?

Characteristics of an Effective Social Studies Classroom

Effective social studies classrooms are active, engaging environments. Students participate in learning experiences that prepare them to be productive, responsible citizens. They gain knowledge about their physical and cultural world and past and present society while participating in learning experiences that enable them to process information in a variety of ways. An effective social studies classroom combines rigor, relevance, and relationships to ensure student mastery of the concepts, contents, and skills that make up the disciplines.

Observing an effective social studies classroom over a period of time would show different things going on every day: a variety of strategies appropriate to the learning, tasks/activities, and objectives. There would be an atmosphere that is engaging, challenging, stimulating, interactive, and thought provoking; lively and alive with student-centered learning, somewhat like a science laboratory. Members of the classroom would be respectful of others' points of view and appreciative of the benefits of diversity. The instruction would be relevant with purposeful learning that focuses on essential questions and understandings that link to other disciplines and the world beyond the classroom walls. A wide variety of resources, technology, visuals, and so on would be available as a means to tap into the varied learning styles of the students. The physical setup would be fluid and flexible and allow for meeting diverse learning needs and styles. Students would be engaged in reading, writing, observing, discussing, presenting, and researching. Collaboration among students would be the norm. Learning would be connected to students' personal experiences, building background knowledge and understanding measured through diagnostic, formative, and summative assessment. The results of those assessments would direct instructional decisions. Most of all, it would be fun!

The question thus becomes "How do I achieve an effective social studies classroom?" Answering that question is the purpose of this book. The chapters that follow are intended to guide and advise the beginning teacher on the journey from novice to master.

This chapter is devoted to planning—the foundation of good instruction. Now that the characteristics of an effective classroom have been defined, it is time to learn about the components to consider when planning for your students and classes.

An Instructional Framework

The instructional framework from Jeffco Public Schools in Golden, Colorado offers a logical way to think about planning instruction. As Figure 1.1 illustrates, there is a constant flow back and forth between each of the components of the framework. A decision in one component affects the decisions that will be made with regard to the other components. Planning is never static; rather, it is a constant ebb and flow of decision making. [Jeffco Public Schools, 2001]

Figure 1.1: Instructional Framework Chart

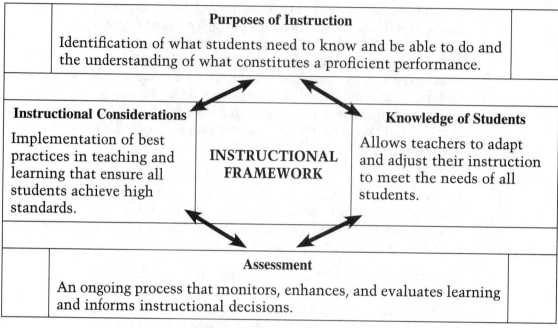

Purposes of Instruction

Identification of what students need to know and be able to do and the understanding of what constitutes a proficient performance.

Instructional Considerations

Implementation of best practices in teaching and learning that ensure all students achieve high standards.

INSTRUCTIONAL FRAMEWORK

Knowledge of Students

Allows teachers to adapt and adjust their instruction to meet the needs of all students.

Assessment

An ongoing process that monitors, enhances, and evaluates learning and informs instructional decisions.

Purposes of Instruction

What do my students need to know and be able to do when instruction (a lesson, unit, etc.) ends and how will the teacher know if they have proficiency in that knowledge and skills? This is the crux of instructional purpose.

Today there are numerous guidelines, documents, and policies that direct the content and skills students are to master in each grade level and each discipline. Perhaps those guidelines are national, state, or local standards. They might be a school or school district's scope and sequence or curriculum guidelines. Whatever form they take, they are the foundation for planning. Granted, the documents often appear ambiguous, repetitive, or just plain confusing. Teachers should solicit help from department heads, instructional leaders, or curriculum coordinators if they are unsure as to the direction their planning needs to take. The majority of schools and school districts have very carefully thought-out plans for implementation that build from grade level to grade level. Often, teachers feel obligated to reteach what students were supposed to have learned in a previous grade or course. Resist the temptation! What tends to happen in that situation is teachers spend so much time catching their students up that they fall behind in teaching what students need to know and be able to do upon leaving their classes, thus perpetuating the never-ending lack of time to teach the assigned curriculum. Instead, activate their background knowledge, enlarge and deepen the understanding of concepts in the context of the content being taught, and help students make connections between what they have learned and what the teacher is teaching. For example, typically students in fifth grade learn about the colonial period in American history and will revisit it again in middle school and high school. Thus, students' first knowledge of colonial settlement is basically at a factual level. Students have learned the facts about colonial settlement, but in middle school, they can begin to understand those facts in an economic or geographic context. For instance, they do not need to relearn the facts; they need to be able to think about them in a different way—a way more appropriate to their cognitive development. Similarly, when they revisit American history in high school, students can think more deeply about that era, perhaps applying what they know of colonization in other parts of the world or in various regions of what would become the United States.

Keep in mind what is known about students and background knowledge in general. Perhaps the 1989 NCSS document, "Charting a Course: Social Studies for the 21st Century" expresses it most effectively:

First, students at all ages know more about the world than is readily apparent. Much of that knowledge represents out-of-school learning . . . Quite young students have rudimentary concepts of some of the critical ideas in social studies: spatial and temporal ordering, authority and power, the nature of groups, cultural differences, scarcity, and many others . . . In particular, the notion that students cannot deal with social studies abstractions until Grade 4 is clearly discredited (Zemelman, Daniels, & Hyde, 1998).

As teachers plan, they should consider the connections they can make from what they are teaching to what students have already learned, in social studies as well as other disciplines. If students have studied earth science, they will have a solid foundation for understanding key geographic concepts. Keep in mind that students may have learned a concept but know it by a different name. Teachers will want to think about the ways they can activate students' background knowledge. As they do so, they should think about their own knowledge of the concepts and content that is being taught. Teachers should ask themselves if they are comfortable with their knowledge and understanding, or if some extra preparation is necessary. Similarly, teachers might ask themselves what they are accountable for in this learning and what accountability belongs to their students? Lastly, what are the resources a teacher will need? How will this teacher use the instructional time to ensure optimum learning?

Knowledge of Students

The more a teacher knows about his or her students in terms of their learning needs and preferences, the more effective that teacher will be in planning instruction. It is not uncommon to have a class of students who arrive with unusual intellect, maturity, and skills when compared with other classes or other years. To offer them the same kind of instruction as those less able or, conversely, to expect a level of performance akin to a particularly gifted group from the less-able group of students results in needless frustration for both the teacher and the students. This is not to say that the teacher should not have high expectations for all of his or her students and offer each of them the very best instruction. Rather, instruction should be geared to their needs, offering them authentic tasks, challenging opportunities, and a variety of ways to learn and demonstrate the knowledge that takes them from where they are and moves them to where they need to be. As previously mentioned, teachers need to consider students' prior knowledge and skills (both what they already have and those they need to be successful). The developmental ages of students and their individual interests or "passions" for a particular content are equally as important. It is quite possible that cultural influences may need to be addressed in instruction. Tall orders to be sure, but manageable if teachers apply the knowledge they have about how students learn.

Thinking about the learning styles of students is another part of planning for effective instruction and working smart. There are numerous resources that explain the components of each learning style and offer various types of instruments for determining each student's learning style. Somewhat surprisingly, students who have taken these assessments and know about the concept of learning styles in general, and what theirs is specifically, demonstrate a new power and responsibility for their own learning. Some students might learn more effectively listening to Martin Luther King Jr.'s I Have a Dream speech rather than (or in addition to) reading it. They might ask to use circles that can be manipulated on the desktop when working with Venn diagrams rather than drawing them on a piece of paper. Certainly students need to be able to play to their strengths in terms of learning style, but also should be encouraged to develop skills that will allow them to take advantage of the other styles that are not their forte. Figure 1.2 summarizes the concept of learning styles.

Teachers have favored learning styles that often translate into a favored teaching style. Students who do not share that learning or teaching style may find themselves at a disadvantage. Therefore, it is incumbent upon teachers to vary their teaching styles in ways that allow all students to learn. The idea of "the guide on the side and not the sage on the stage" is a well-known maxim, one that is perhaps a bit trite. However, teachers who employ that "guide on the side" philosophy in their planning are better able to address the varied learning styles of their students, which in turn, results in students who are more successful.

Figure 1.2: Learning Styles

What are learning styles? Simply put, they are different approaches or ways of learning.

What are the types of learning styles? Commonly, three different styles of learning are identified.

Visual Learners—*learn through seeing* . . . Visual learners need to see the teacher's body language and facial expression to fully understand the content of a lesson. They tend to prefer sitting at the front of the classroom to avoid visual obstructions (e.g., people's heads). They may think in pictures and learn best from visual displays including: diagrams, illustrated textbooks, overhead transparencies, videos, flipcharts, and handouts. During a lecture or classroom discussion, visual learners often prefer to take detailed notes to absorb the information.

Auditory Learners—*learn through listening* . . . Auditory learners learn best through verbal lectures, discussions, talking things through, and listening to what others have to say. Auditory learners interpret the underlying meanings of speech through listening to tone of voice, pitch, speed, and other nuances. Written information may have little meaning until it is heard. These learners often benefit from reading text aloud and using a tape recorder.

Tactile/Kinesthetic Learners—*learn through moving, doing and touching* . . . Tactile/Kinesthetic learners learn best through a hands-on approach, actively exploring the physical world around them. They may find it hard to sit still for long periods and may become distracted by their need for activity and exploration.

Conceived by Howard Gardner, multiple intelligences offer seven different ways to approach learning and demonstrate understanding. Closely related to learning styles, the intelligences recognize that students have a variety of innate abilities or intelligences that can aid in their learning if they are provided opportunities to demonstrate their understanding in different ways. For example, instead of taking a pencil-and-paper test or writing an essay, a student may choose to write lyrics (and perhaps even the music) to a song that illustrates a particular concept.

Roger Taylor (1994) uses intelligences to guide him in placing students in cooperative groups. Imagine the workings of a collaborative group of seven students, each representing a particular intelligence where the tasks necessary to complete a given project reflect each intelligence. The student with strong interpersonal intelligence can use those skills to manage the group, ensuring all are on task, that deadlines are met, and any details are taken care of. Visual aspects of the project are completed under the guidance of the student with visual/spatial intelligence. Leadership for the written requirement of the project belongs to the verbal/linguistic-gifted child, etc. Students with an understanding of their intelligences come to a collaborative group knowing that they have something unique to offer to the group that will be of value in completing the assignment. Consider, too, the grading of the group—the bane of many teachers who like students to work collaboratively. If the task is constructed in such a way as to use each student's strength, then evaluating a project becomes a much simpler and pleasant process.

Not to be overlooked in knowing your students is the idea of relationship. Teachers have always known that students who enjoy their classes show a greater willingness to engage in the learning and demonstrate higher achievement. Not to be confused with popularity, a teacher's positive relationship with students is an important component to a student's success in school. Students who know their teachers care about their learning, care about them as individuals, and care enough to hold them to high levels of expectation generally enjoy that teacher's class and do well as a result.

Assessment

An in-depth discussion of assessment can be found in Chapter 10; however, it is a critical component of any instructional framework and must be considered when planning. Assessment plays into each aspect of instruction, whether it monitors progress, enhances and evaluates learning, or informs instructional decisions. As previously mentioned, teachers should know their students. Part of that knowing is assessing background knowledge, along with students' strengths and weaknesses, in order to design lessons that address varied learning styles and multiple intelligences.

Teachers assess student progress daily, most often in an informal manner. They look at body language and facial expressions, and listen to how students react to their teaching. Those elements are a form of assessment and inform teachers in an immediate way as to whether their students are "getting it" or not. Those cues, for accomplished teachers, determine what happens next in a classroom. For example, accomplished teachers teach a lesson the first hour and are mentally "tweaking" the lesson to be presented in the next class period. This process continues, almost automatically, as the teacher continues through the day, making the changes in instruction necessary to help students learn.

As teachers begin their planning, they should be clear on what it is they want their students to know and be able to do. With that goal in place, how can teachers measure that learning? How will they know students have met the learning goals set forth in the lesson? How will they communicate that information to students in such a way that they are able to understand what is necessary to enhance their learning and improve their demonstration of it? How will they explain that information to parents? How will teachers change their instruction to meet the needs of students who do not demonstrate proficiency in the skills or content they have taught them? What venues will teachers provide for students to assess their own learning? How will they ensure that students have a variety of ways to demonstrate their learning (capitalizing on their learning styles and intelligences)? What will their rubric look like? Will it allow for continuous monitoring of progress and instruction?

Clearly, assessment is a key component to instruction. The most effective teachers are assessing student learning constantly and making instructional decisions based on those assessments.

Instructional Considerations

The fourth and final component to the instructional framework is instructional considerations. This aspect of the instructional framework is wide-ranging and multidimensional. Four components are classroom management and environment, the teacher, the student, and instruction. At the start of this chapter, an effective social studies classroom was defined. In that scenario, there were many examples of what is referred to as "best practices." Zemelman, Daniels, and Hyde (1998) discuss best practices in all content areas in their book of the same name. They recommend increasing the following practices in your social studies classroom:

- in-depth study of topics in each social studies field in which students make choices about what to study and discover the complexities of human interaction

- emphasis on activities that engage students in inquiry and problem solving about significant human issues

- participation in interactive and cooperative classroom study processes that bring together students of all ability levels

- integration of social studies with other areas of the curriculum

- richer content in elementary grades, building on the prior knowledge children bring to social studies topics; includes study of concepts from psychology, sociology, economics, and political science, as well as history and geography; understand, within their experience, American social institutions, issues for social groups, and problems of everyday living

- students' valuing and sense of connection with American and global history, the history and culture of diverse social groups, and the environment that surrounds them

- students' inquiry about the cultural groups they belong to and other cultural groups represented in their school and community in order to promote the students' sense of ownership in the social studies curriculum

- use of evaluation that involves further learning and that promotes responsible citizenship and open expression of ideas

Teachers will notice that many of the topics in the context of the instructional framework are reflected in the list of best practices. All the bulleted items support the idea of students actively involved in their own learning, and offer a variety of ways that this can be accomplished.

When thinking about a classroom environment that employs the social studies best practices, one must also think about the management of such a classroom. To an untrained eye, the activities and activeness of students in such a classroom may appear chaotic, but there is a great deal of difference between unmanaged chaos and carefully constructed and planned lessons that depend on students working in groups or independently on a variety of tasks simultaneously. Granted, those classrooms are noisy and in constant motion with students talking to one another and moving desks or tables to facilitate the work they are doing. But they are also the classrooms where students are engaged in learning, completing tasks they view as relevant to their lives, and depending on one another for collegial thinking, sharing, and support. At the center of all this activity is the teacher who has meticulously planned the lesson (and is really guiding from the side) by moving throughout the classroom, constantly monitoring the work that is going on, offering advice when needed, and serving as a valuable resource.

Certainly it is unrealistic to think that each best practice will be used during each class period, but consciously including them in planning and using them with greater frequency will support a classroom environment that is rich in learning and student involvement.

Conclusion

Teachers are better versed in and more knowledgeable about learning and teaching than they were 25 years ago. While at times overwhelming, the latest research provides educators with an incredible amount of information about how best to teach students. Kati Haycock (1998) of the Education Trust writes extensively about the importance of the teacher, the uncontested determinant of student success in learning. As noted at the start of this chapter, planning is the foundation of good instruction. Teachers who master the skill of planning are the type of teachers about whom Haycock writes.

Additional Resources

Daniels, H., & Bizar, M. (1998). *Methods that matter.* York, Maine: Stenhouse Publishers.

Wolf, P. (2001). *Brain Matters.* Alexandria, VA: Association for Supervision and Curriculum Development.

Chapter 1 Reflection

1. What would a lesson that allows a student to capitalize on his or her preferred learning style look like?

_____

_____

_____

_____

2. How will you develop positive relationships with students so each student will be successful?

_____

_____

_____

_____

_____

3. What kind of a learner/teacher are you and how will you adapt your learning/teaching style to address the various styles of your students?

_____

_____

_____

_____

_____

_____

Building Background Knowledge

In the social studies, students need to learn a huge amount of content. Robert Marzano (2004) concludes from a wealth of research that what students will learn is based on what they already know. In other words, learning new content is strongly tied to their background knowledge about a subject.

Children certainly come to school with background knowledge that is experiential. However, students often come to school with no background knowledge about topics that teachers must teach. They lack academic background knowledge. There are also discrepancies between the background knowledge of impoverished children and those who are fortunate enough to come from families who provide rich language development experiences. Research indicates that since background knowledge is a predictor of success in school, schools and teachers must strategically build background knowledge (Marzano, 2004).

With this in mind then, a critical question for teachers is how should they introduce topics and concepts so that their students will be able to learn the content of the disciplines. Since the correlation between vocabulary knowledge and academic achievement is high, this chapter and the next chapter will emphasize vocabulary. This chapter will focus on how to build background knowledge, including strategies for building vocabulary skills. Chapter 3 will focus specifically on teaching key vocabulary.

Very few seventh graders come to school knowing about the Spanish American War. Other students may have heard about World War II or the Vietnam War but their knowledge is vague. Young children may know a little about American Indians, but come to school with the misinformation that all Indians live in teepees. Therefore it is important for teachers to first find out what students know in order to guide their instruction. Teachers also must provide students with a framework of understanding so they can better access new information. Additionally, teachers want to capture imaginations so students will be eager to learn. As discussed in Chapter 1, teachers want to provide students with academically enriching experiences to enhance background knowledge. However, when direct experiences such as field trips are not possible, teachers must provide those experiences in the classroom.

The strategies that follow are effective tools for helping students build background knowledge.

Picture Walks

An excellent way to help students build background knowledge is to conduct a picture walk. Consider the example of an elementary unit on ancient Rome. Before students study the history and culture of ancient Rome, they must learn about the geography of the region and its impact on the people. To introduce the unit, collect a wide variety of books on many different reading levels. Place these around the room at different stations. Have students rotate through the stations in small groups and scan the books, looking for pictures of geographical features. They may record notes about what they see, or draw pictures of the geography. They will also discover other aspects of the culture as they explore the books. After students have rotated through the stations, bring them together as a group and discuss what they observed. Focusing first on the geography, create a visual chart that shows the students' observations. Next, students should make predictions about aspects of daily life in ancient Rome. If students have studied other cultures such as the ancient Greeks or Aztecs, comparisons will be made. How did the people adapt to their environments? What were their lives like? The responses of the students can be recorded on the chart. At this point, it is also important to encourage the students to ask questions. These questions encourage students to be active learners and should be used to guide further investigations.

Advanced Organizers

Many upper-elementary students study their state governments in their state history classes. One way of introducing the structure of the government is to begin by asking the students what they know about government. Some may have background knowledge about the national government. Many have information about the current president or other presidents in our history.

They may be familiar with elections and the court system. They may also know that the government makes laws and perhaps that it provides services. As the students discuss what they know, the teacher can record the information on the board.

Then, the teacher will introduce the structure of the state government by displaying an advanced organizer similar to the one in Figure 2.1. Preview with the students what they will be studying. Discuss the words *executive*, *legislative*, and *judicial* and explain in very basic terminology the responsibilities of each branch. Then, explain that the state has a governor, legislature, and court system. Deliberately make the connection that most state-government structures parallel the structure of the federal government. Students need to know that a governor of a state is similar to the president of the nation. This simple graphic will give students some background knowledge and a pictorial organizer before they begin reading text materials. As the study of the state branches of government proceeds, information can be added to the graphic to further refine and elaborate on the roles of each branch. It is also suggested that the teacher and students add pictures or icons in the advanced organizer to provide another aid for memory retention.

Figure 2.1: Advanced Organizer for Government

	Executive	Legislative	Judicial
Federal Government			
State Government			

Using Picture Books

Picture books can be used effectively with students of all age groups (not just elementary students) and are excellent tools for introducing a topic or unit. Using these books is particularly effective when the students do not have background knowledge. Reading a picture book gives everyone in the class a base of information. The visuals are engaging and immediately draw students into the story. It is also fun to see the reaction of students who are familiar with books they read as very young children and now must view them in a different context. When introducing a picture book, first ask if students know anything about the topic. Then, have them consider the book title and cover illustrations to make predictions about the content. A brief amount of time should be allowed for the students to skim the pictures and make further predictions. Often, multiple copies of the book are available from school libraries, and students can work in small groups to make their predictions. After the book has been read aloud by the teacher, students can share impressions and generate questions that can be used to guide instruction.

There are a myriad of books for primary units, but these are some favorites for introducing units that typically belong to middle school and high school social studies.

- *Casey Over There* by Staton Rabin—World War I
- *The Butter Battle Book* by Dr. Seuss—The Cold War
- *Mercedes and the Chocolate Pilot* by Margo Raven—Berlin Airlift
- *Pie Biter* by Ruthanne McCunn—Transcontinental Railroad (written in Spanish, English, and Chinese)
- *Seaman's Journal: On the Trail with Lewis and Clark* by Patricia Reeder Eubank—U.S. expansion
- *George Did It* by Suzanne Tripp Jurmain—Setting precedent for the presidency
- *The Great Migration* by Jacob Lawrence— Migration of African Americans from the South to the North, beginning around World War I

Tea Party Strategy

The Tea Party is an engaging prereading strategy that helps students activate background knowledge, anticipate what they will read, make predictions before they read, and make connections to information they already know. It also gets the students out of their desks and talking to one another as if they are mingling at a tea party.

To set up the Tea Party, select eight to ten statements from the text that will be read. Write these statements on index cards, repeating statements to match the number of students in the class. After distributing one card to each student, he or she is then given a chance to read the statement silently. Then they all stand and mingle. Their jobs are to move about the classroom and read the statement on their index cards to as many other classmates as possible. The only conversation taking place is the reading of the index cards. After a few minutes, students meet in small groups of their own choosing to discuss what they surmise about the text from the statements. In their groups, they make predictions and list questions. The goal is to anticipate what will be read. The students then read the text to check the accuracy of their predictions and answer their questions.

Word Webs

A word web is a visual organizer to help students build background knowledge. Look at the example of introducing a unit on American Indians, Figure 2.2. In preparation for the discussion, the teacher categorizes the material that will need to be covered, such as clothing, shelter, transportation, and food; and creates a blank web. The students are then asked, "What do you know about American Indians?" As they respond, the teacher writes the words in the appropriate categories. It is important that the teacher accept any responses that the students share. It is appropriate to list incorrect information that will be clarified and corrected as the unit progresses.

Figure 2.2: American Indian Web

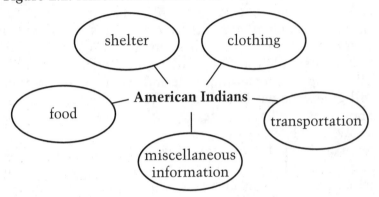

A teacher might also take another approach to building the word web. Depending on the needs and abilities of the students, a teacher might not provide any categories. The students may begin by listing information that they know about American Indians and these words can be written on cards. As the words are discussed, students may generate their own categories. With either technique, the teacher should leave the webs up throughout the unit so that students can revisit the words, adding information and correcting misconceptions.

List, Group, Label

List, Group, Label (Taba, 1967) is a good technique for building background knowledge and for finding out what students already know about a topic. A teacher creates a list of essential words that will be used in a unit. The words are written on sets of cards and copies of the same set are distributed to small groups of students who will discuss and categorize them. Working in groups, students are asked to categorize the words and explain the reasons they categorized as they did. Students defend their choices of categories and learn from one another.

In an introductory unit on the causes and events lead-ing to the Revolutionary War, use the following words: *taxes*, *Stamp Act*, *boycott*, *England*, *American colo-nies*, *Patriot*, *Loyalist*, *King George III*, *Patrick Henry*, *Thomas Jefferson*, *George Washington*, *independence*, *John Locke*, *French and Indian War*, *representation*, and *Declaration of Independence*. In this case, each group of students will probably create very different categories. One group may focus on people and events while another will group the words by leaders, terms, and documents. They may also have a category, titled, *Words We Do Not Know*. Each group will record its categories on chart paper and explain its reasoning. The charts with the categories will be saved and revisited as students learn about the causes and events leading to the Revolutionary War. Students may revise their categorizations and add other words as their study progresses.

Rate Your Knowledge

Rate Your Knowledge is a graphic organizer that is used prior to reading text to assess students' familiarity with words and give them a purpose for reading. It also helps students build their confidence before reading because they recognize the words before beginning the text. To begin, select no more than 10 words from a piece of text that students should read. Choose the words carefully, considering which are central to understanding the text or which may cause problems for the students. Create a chart such as Figure 2.3. After distributing a copy to each student, read the words aloud. Then, ask students to rate their familiarity with the words. During or after reading, the students generate a content-specific defini-tion of the unknown or unfamiliar words. Discuss the words upon completion of the reading to ensure that students understand each word.

Figure 2.3: Rate Your Knowledge

Word	Can use the word in a sentence	Have seen or heard the word	Don't know the word	Meaning after reading

In another version of Rate Your Knowledge, the teacher finds the words in the context of the reading selection and writes the sentences from the reading that contain the words in the left-hand column. The key vocabulary word is underlined in each example. By giving students a context, they may be able to make some inferences about the meaning of the word before they tackle the text.

Predicting ABCs

Predicting ABCs (Allen, 1999) helps students activate and build background knowledge and make predictions about the content of the material they will be reading. It also helps set a purpose for reading. Before reading an article, primary source, or textbook chapter, preview the text and pick significant words and concepts that the students should know.

For a unit on the civil rights movement, plan to have students read an article about the integration of public schools. Write the title of the article or text on the board or overhead. Briefly discuss the title and meaning of the words in the title. Then, distribute Figure 2.4. Using the overhead, model brainstorming some words that might be related to the topic and put those words in the appropriate box. Teachers may put words such as *African Americans* in the A–B block, *sit-ins* in the S–T block, and *integration* in the I–J block. Have students then work in pairs to brainstorm other words they think might appear in the reading. Ask them to share these words with the class and add them to the chart on the overhead. Then, have the students read the text and look for the words in their predictions. As they read, they should add other important words from the text. They should be able to justify the reasons that they added the words during the discussion.

In another variation of this strategy, prior to reading, students might only focus on a few of the letters. Teachers may want them to begin with the letters A, B, E, I, and S. The teacher has picked these letters, because the article is about brave African American students, *Brown v. Board of Education*, education, integration, struggles in southern states, sit-ins, and schools. Once students have read the material, they can add other words, in the appropriate boxes, that they feel are important.

Figure 2.4: Predicting ABCs

A–B African Americans	C–D	E–F	G–H
I–J integration	K–L	M–N	O–P
Q–R	S–T sit-ins	U–V	W–Z

Wordsplash

Another good strategy for activating background knowledge before reading text is Wordsplash conceived by W. Dorsey Hammond, a professor of education at Salisbury University. It draws upon students' background knowledge, asks them to make predictions about what the text will be about, requires them to make connections among the words, and generates interest. In this case, the teacher reads the content material of the lesson and picks out 10 key words or important concepts from the text to be read. These words are then arranged randomly on paper and reproduced for handouts. A sample for the Silk Road is shown in Figure 2.5. Working in groups, students examine the words and predict how the words are related to one another and to the topic under study. Before reading the text, they write the statements showing the relationships among the words. They then read the text with the purpose of seeing if their predictions are accurate. Even if the predictions are inaccurate, the strategy gives students opportunities to analyze their preconceived notions and integrate them with the new information that has been learned. Following the reading, students can then revise their statements to include accurate information as well as to add important information that would refine their understanding of the words and elaborate upon the relationships among the words.

A more detailed explanation of this strategy can be found in *Reading Strategies for Social Studies* (by Stephanie Macceca, Shell Education, 2007).

Figure 2.5: Wordsplash for the Silk Road

caravans   spices
        Marco Polo

              Silk Road

            trade
                              Mongols
      China
                  precious goods
                                    travelers
      politics
                      religion

Conclusion

It is essential that social studies teachers use strategies to activate and build background knowledge. What students already know about a topic is one of the strongest indicators of how well they will be able to learn new information. As a colleague once said, when students encounter new information, they need a pocket to put it in. In other words, they need to have a way of organizing the information and integrating it with what they already know. Once they have some prior knowledge, they are better able to learn the new information.

Additional Resources

Macceca, S. (2007). *Reading Strategies for Social Studies*. Huntington Beach, CA: Shell Education.

Ogle, D., Klemp, R., & McBride, B. (2007). *Building literacy in social studies*. Alexandria, VA: ASCD.

Chapter 2 Reflection

1. As an adult learner, think of a subject matter that is very difficult for you to learn. What kind of background knowledge do you need in order to learn and understand information about this subject? How could you relate your experiences to those of your students?

_____

_____

_____

_____

2. What strategies do you employ for building background knowledge for your diverse student population, especially English language learners?

_____

_____

_____

_____

3. Think of a unit that you will be teaching soon. What knowledge do students need to make sense of the material? Describe at least one strategy you use to help them develop this knowledge.

_____

_____

_____

_____

Strategies for Teaching Vocabulary

As discussed in Chapter 2, vocabulary is integrally linked with background knowledge. Key vocabulary is introduced in the activities previously described. However, once students have built some background knowledge, teachers must move on to teaching words and concepts explicitly. "Systematic vocabulary instruction is one of the most important instructional interventions that teachers can use, particularly with low-achieving students" (Marzano, Pickering, & Pollock, 2001). In addition to building background knowledge, explicit vocabulary instruction increases reading comprehension, helps students communicate more effectively, improves the range and specificity of student writing, enables students to communicate more effectively, and helps students develop a deeper understanding of concepts (Allen, 1999).

The social studies discipline has a unique vocabulary and therefore, teachers must build vocabulary instruction into their planning. "Teaching words well entails helping students make connections between their prior knowledge and the vocabulary to be encountered in the text and providing them with multiple opportunities to clarify and extend their knowledge of words and concepts during the course of study" (Vacca, 1999, p. 319). With so much vocabulary in social studies, where do teachers begin? It is important to focus on specific words that are important for what students will be learning. While teachers cannot teach all the content words students need to know, they must strategically pick a few that are essential for understanding major concepts in a unit.

Looking up words and writing their definitions does not help students learn vocabulary. Instead, teachers must provide a variety of opportunities for students to interact with words. Janet Allen (1999) advises that words be used in a meaningful context between 10 and 15 times. The latest research also advises (Marzano, Pickering, & Pollack, 2001) that students should create pictures and other graphic representations of words, be able to compare and contrast words, classify them, and create metaphors and analogies. They should discuss words and play with them.

Word Walls

Word walls can be seen in many classrooms from primary to high school level. For the purposes of this book, the focus will be the use of content word walls that help develop academic vocabulary. Some word walls are arranged in alphabetical order while others are arranged by topic. However, it is not enough to just have words posted in the classroom; rather, word walls must be made interactive. As a teacher introduces the content of a unit, key vocabulary words are carefully chosen and gradually added to the walls (Allen, 1999). The words are posted and visible throughout a given unit, and students should refer to them often to use them in their discussion and writing. The words should also be displayed on cards so students can easily manipulate them and make connections between the words. For instance, students could

- sort and classify them in various ways;
- regroup words when they look for cause and effect;
- look for ways to compare and contrast words;
- find synonyms and antonyms;
- examine positive and negative connotations;
- use them in journal entries;
- create picture dictionaries;
- identify what they each think is the "most important" word and tell why;
- explain a word's importance to a unit of study.

When words are used in warm-up exercises or at the end of lessons, teachers also have an excellent informal assessment tool.

Words in Context (Word Meaning)

This technique helps students explore key concept words. A graphic organizer (Figure 3.1) was designed by Janet Allen (1999) to enable students to develop a deeper meaning of an important concept. When students study world cultures or some specific period in American history, they must understand the economic concept of interdependence. At the beginning of a unit of study, a teacher would discuss interdependence by creating an overhead of the graphic organizer and writing interdependence in the central box. An example is shown in Figure 3.1. With the teacher leading the discussion, students can look at the word in a sentence or create a definition for it to be placed in the top box. As the students talk about what it is and what it is not, the teacher fills in the ovals and boxes on each side of the word. Students will then discuss specific examples from their unit of study and be able to give examples from both their previous study as well as connect the concept to their own lives. The graphic organizer can be revisited throughout the unit, and as students make connections and find additional examples, they will add that information to the organizer.

Figure 3.1: Words in Context

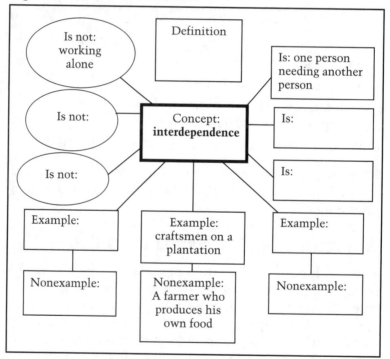

Adapted from vocabulary word map by Raymond Jones at http://www.readingquest.org.

Another graphic organizer has similar components to Figure 3.1, but may be a little easier and can be used very effectively with English language learners and special education students because it incorporates the use of pictures. Research says that nonlinguistic representations are effective in helping students think about their learning and in remembering information (Marzano, Pickering, & Pollock, 2001). With the graphic pictured in Figure 3.2, students combine both linguistic and non-linguistic tools to learn a concept. They need to find synonyms and antonyms for a word, use the word in a meaningful way, and draw a picture of it. This organizer can be created by students and used for assessment.

Figure 3.2: Vocabulary Word Map

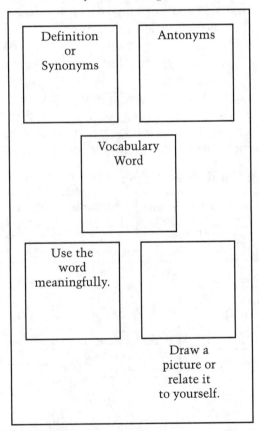

Adapted from vocabulary word map by Raymond Jones at http://www.readingquest.org.

Word Questioning

Word questioning asks students to demonstrate higher levels of thinking. It employs Bloom's taxonomy to help students analyze, comprehend, apply, synthesize, demonstrate knowledge, and evaluate what they know about a particular concept. Consider a unit on the post-Civil War era. Figure 3.3 shows the graphic organizer for the word *Reconstruction*. A sentence from a textbook or a sentence that the teacher constructs would be placed in the central box of the graphic organizer. Then, students work from the remaining boxes to see what parts of the word they might recognize. They can make a prediction about the meaning of the word before giving examples of what it is and what it is not. Then, students make connections to what they already know. They think about when, where, and under what circumstances they would find the word and finally evaluate its importance.

Figure 3.3: Word Questioning

How does this word fit with other words and concepts I know?
After wars, people need to rebuild their lives.

What makes this an important word for me to know?
What happened after the Civil War in the South?

Are these parts of the word I recognize?
re-, construct

It is . . . building again

Reconstruction began after the Civil War ended.

I think this word means . . . rebuilding

It is not . . .
tearing something down

When, where, and under what conditions might I find this word?
- in studying the period after the Civil War
- when we discussed rebuilding after Katrina
- when we discuss what will happen after a modern day war

Frayer Model

The Frayer Model (Frayer, Frederick, & Klausmeier, 1969) is another strategy that helps students understand concepts and is an excellent graphic organizer that can be used as a basis for writing even with the youngest of students. It allows students to see what a concept is and what it is not. Students also demonstrate their understanding by providing examples and non-examples. Possible topics for a civics class might include: the Articles of Confederation, the First Amendment, democracy, or communism. Figure 3.4 is an example using the concept of a dictatorship. Students define the topic in their own words, list essential characteristics, and then add examples and non-examples. They may also draw pictures in the four boxes. In a variation of this model, students write the essential characteristics of the topic in the top left-hand box and nonessential characteristics in the top right-hand box. Students can also place examples and non-examples in the bottom right-hand box and use the bottom left-hand box for an illustration.

Figure 3.4: Frayer Model

Definition One person runs a whole country all by himself.	Essential Characteristics • Government controlled by one person • Little or no individual freedom • Rule by force or threat • Not a democracy • Not a republic
Examples • North Korea • Nazi Germany	Non-examples • The United States • South Korea • Germany today

dictatorship

Making Comparisons

Another good vocabulary activity that helps students learn terms and concepts is one in which they must compare and contrast information. Research confirms that one of the most effective ways for students to retain content information is to have them make comparisons between ideas (Marzano, Pickering, & Pollock, 2001). Many teachers use a Venn diagram, but other graphic organizers can be more effective and easy to use. When U.S. history students study the new republic, they must examine the emergence of political parties. The H-diagram in Figure 3.5 shows a comparison between the Federalists and Democratic Republicans. As students examine the critical information about the two parties, they list the differences on the two sides of the *H* and the similarities in the crossbar. Certainly, this graphic organizer can be used to compare important historical figures or other abstract terms. Ogle, Klemp, and McBride (2007) also suggest using a Y–chart to illustrate differences and similarities between terms. Students list differences between two concepts or terms in the top part of the Y and the similarities in the base of the Y.

Figure 3.5: H-diagram for Comparisons

Federalists
Led by Hamilton
Strong central government
Loose interpretation of the Constitution
Wanted large peacetime army
National bank
Pro tariffs
Supported by northern businessmen and large landowners

Similarities
Political party
Had a vision for the new nation

Democratic Republicans
Led by Jefferson
Weak central government
Strict interpretation of the Constitution
Wanted small peacetime army
No national bank
Against tariffs
Supported by skilled workers, small farmers, and plantation owners

Concept Circles

Once teachers have taught various words, how do they know if students have learned them and can use them meaningfully? Chapter 10 makes suggestions for informal assessments, and all of the strategies discussed in this chapter can be used for assessment of understanding. Another easy technique for assessment is the use of concept circles (Vacca & Vacca, 1999). Figure 3.6 shows a circle divided into four parts, but it can be divided into six or even eight parts, depending on the concept. With concept circles, students must know the meaning of the words in the sections, analyze the relationship among the words, and think of the concept that ties the words together. In this example, the concept is the Great Plains. Students understand that inventions and new tools improved life for settlers on the Great Plains in the 1800s.

Figure 3.6: Concept Circle

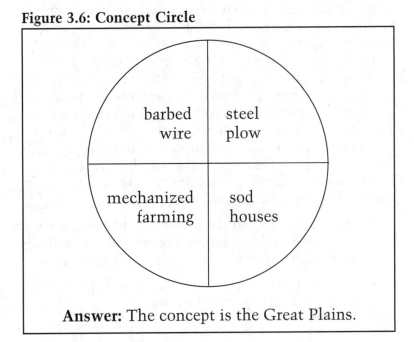

Answer: The concept is the Great Plains.

There are other variations in using concept circles. In one variation, a teacher can give students a circle that has words in three sections and one blank section. Again, students must know the meanings of the three words, understand their relationships to one another, and identify the concept. Then, they must add a fourth word in the blank section that also relates in a similar way to the concept. In a second variation, a teacher can give students a blank organizer but tell them the concept. Students then need to fill in the sections of the circle with words that describe the concept. They then must justify how the words are related to the concept.

Figuring Out Words in Context

The previous strategies help students understand the meaning of concept words. However, teachers certainly cannot analyze every new word that students encounter or even teach all of the words that students do not know. So, how can teachers help children become independent learners and figure out new words from context? Often, when students encounter new words, they just skip them. Unfortunately, that strategy does not serve learners well. Teachers must give students the strategies for figuring out new words in context. As the teacher reads a passage orally or as students tackle difficult text, they should be aware of the strategies they are using to figure out new words. Teachers can model by using the following ways to help students understand new words in context. (Allen & Landaker, 2005, pp. 45–47)

- Often, students can figure out a word because they have some background knowledge and can infer its meaning from what they already know.

- Suffixes, prefixes, and root words can help students determine word meaning.

- Sometimes the clue to the meaning of the word is right in the sentence. Signal words alert the reader to the definition of the word. Signal words might include *for example* or *including*. At other times, the author will restate the word or use words such as *in other words* or *also called*. Words like *consequently* or *because* signal a cause-and-effect relationship. Comparisons may be signaled by *like* or *similar to* and contrasts may be signaled by *but, however*, and *in contrast*.

- Finally, students should look all around the word. Graphs, titles, pictures and footnotes all help students find the meaning of new vocabulary.

Conclusion

Much is written on the importance of vocabulary instruction. Social studies teachers must explicitly teach words, bearing in mind that they must choose the most important words and concepts in the discipline. Students also need to make connections between what they know and what they must learn. They must study related words and have multiple opportunities to use their new vocabulary words. Students need opportunities to represent words linguistically and non-linguistically, to talk about the words, and to have fun with them.

Additional Resources

Blanchowicz, C. (2005). *Teaching vocabulary in all classrooms.* Upper Saddle River, NJ: Prentice Hall.

Tompkins, G. (2007). *Teaching vocabulary: 50 creative strategies, grades 6–12.* Upper Saddle River, NJ: Prentice Hall.

Chapter 3 Reflection

1. How will a focus on vocabulary help your students?

   _____

   _____

   _____

   _____

2. In what unit do you think the vocabulary is most challenging for your students? What techniques will you try that explicitly teach key vocabulary for this unit?

   _____

   _____

   _____

   _____

   _____

3. Use the Internet to find other strategies for teaching vocabulary. Which interest you? How could you use them for your group of students?

   _____

   _____

   _____

   _____

   _____

   _____

   _____

Making Sense of Nonfiction

This chapter will address making sense of text. Through reading, students are provided with windows on the past and windows on contemporary cultures. If teachers want students to become actively engaged with their content, students need to read widely, write about what they learn (including using graphic or visual representations), and verbalize their thoughts.

Entire books are written on the topic of reading in the content area. Nevertheless, this topic is addressed in this book because reading and comprehending text are critical to the study of history and society. Social studies teachers are not trained to be reading teachers. However, teachers must give students the tools to make meaning from text. Teachers cannot take it for granted that students come to school equipped with good comprehension skills. Therefore, is it imperative that teachers model thinking aloud and give students multiple opportunities to develop and use comprehension skills. Teachers should provide a variety of reading materials on different reading levels and in a variety of formats. In a social studies class, teachers must give students a purpose for reading and engage them with content. Students also need help actively interacting with texts as they read as well as reflecting on what they have read. This chapter will address a few key strategies for previewing and interacting with text. Social studies teachers always ask students to find important information and main ideas, make inferences, and summarize, so those skills will be another focus of the chapter.

In the social studies, students must interact with a huge array of text. In the primary grades, they learn to read a variety of nonfiction trade books. Then in about fourth grade, they begin to read textbooks. As they advance through grades, their textbooks become much more complex and challenging, and students must also read from a variety of other sources.

Many content reading books for teachers divide their information into three categories: pre-reading strategies, during-reading strategies, and post-reading strategies. For the purposes of this book, these strategies will not be divided so concretely because one strategy may overlap categories.

Turning Headings into Questions

It is important to give students a purpose for reading. To do this, begin with a pre-reading strategy that can be used effectively with all ages of students, including those in the primary grades. This pre-reading strategy also draws on the interests of students and makes them active participants in their own learning. A third-grade teacher wants to introduce a nonfiction trade book to her students because they are studying ancient Greece. One of the chapter titles is "Athena's City." The teacher begins by having students look at the pictures in the chapter. Then, students are reminded of question words such as *who, what, when, where, why,* and *how.* Students generate questions about the chapter and the teacher lists them on the board. They might ask, "Who was Athena?" "What city was named after her?" "Why would a city be called Athena's City?" If there's a picture of the Parthenon, students might be interested in comparing what it looks like now to a drawing depicting it long ago. Depending on the reading abilities of the students, they can read the short chapter independently or in pairs, or the teacher can read the chapter aloud. Answers to the student-generated questions are listed on the board following the reading. If the questions are not answered by the text, this is an excellent opportunity for the teacher to encourage students to read further and consult other sources to find those answers. The initial questions may also generate additional questions that will engage the student learners.

Previewing Texts

Textbooks often overwhelm students because of the quantity of information, challenging academic vocabulary, and vast breadth of content. Some of these textbooks may not be written in a very engaging manner, and often students come to the textbook with little or no background knowledge. The publishers of these books have incorporated text supports to help students understand content. These include headings and subheadings; visuals such as diagrams, graphs, and charts; time lines; focus questions; introductions; keywords in bold, italics or color; and pictures. Before students can understand the content, teachers must help them understand the purpose of these supports (Allen & Landaker, 2005).

At the beginning of a school year, provide a blank template of the introductory page of a textbook chapter (Ogle, Klemp, & McBride, 2007). The blank template includes empty boxes or drawings of the main features of the textbook page that mirror the page and might look like Figure 4.1. The page might include a sidebar that lists a key question or big idea for the chapter and important vocabulary, a time line and an introductory paragraph follow a chapter title, a subheading leads to more text, and a picture with a caption is in the lower left-hand corner of the page. Students can work with partners to match the text supports with the blank template and label the template with words from the text. It is then essential to discuss each text feature and help students understand the purpose of the feature and how each feature can help them understand the organization and content in the text.

Figure 4.1: Previewing the Textbook

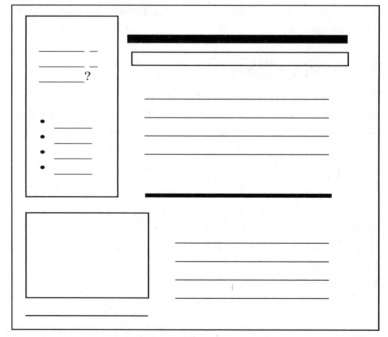

Paired Reading

In many classrooms, it is common to see students taking turns reading aloud from their textbooks. When one student finishes a section, another begins reading. There are times when having one student read a passage aloud while others listen is appropriate. However, a teacher needs to ask, what are the other students doing while one is reading? Are all students focused on the passage? Are they just waiting for their turns to read? Are they looking at the book while thinking of something else? Paired reading is an interactive strategy in which all of the students are more involved. In this activity, students read aloud and talk about the reading with partners. When the strategy is first introduced, select a short passage or paragraph for the students to read. Pair the students. Have one student read the text aloud. When the first student has completed the passage, the second student summarizes what has been read and adds supporting details. The second student can also ask questions of the reader. When the pairs have read and discussed their initial reading, they switch roles and the second student reads while the first summarizes, adds details, and asks questions. In this way, all students in the class are actively involved in the reading. The teacher will bring the students together for a class discussion and everyone can share what they have learned. As students become more proficient with the process, longer sections of text can be assigned.

In addition to paired reading, teachers might group the students in triads. If a student struggles with reading, he or she can always assume the role of active listener and still be responsible for asking questions and summarizing. In addition to reading a textbook, students can be paired to read different materials. They may be reading informational texts such as newspaper articles, primary sources, other textbooks, or encyclopedias. The materials will also be on different reading levels to accommodate for differences in the learning needs of students. If a variety of text materials are used, it is important that students share with the entire class what they have learned. This way, everyone benefits from this new information, and everyone, regardless of ability level, has the chance to teach others something new.

Reader's Theater

Reader's theater is a reading activity that builds fluency. Students do not have to memorize lines, but they build their confidence for reading while learning social studies content. In this activity, students write their own scripts and perform them for the class. Students are divided into pairs and copies of historical documents or text are provided to read and interpret. The reading materials need to present two viewpoints for comparison and contrast. The teacher provides students with guiding questions and a clear format for them to follow. Students read for information and then write for understanding.

In this example, consider reading material on the viewpoints of the Patriots and Loyalists during the Revolutionary War. Depending on student reading levels and lesson objectives, they could read their textbook materials, primary source letters, or fictional accounts. The teacher would ensure that each student had materials that they could read successfully. One member of the pair would have material on the Patriot viewpoint and the other would have the Loyalist viewpoint. Guiding questions might include:

- What is your view of the laws made by Great Britain?
- Why are people fighting the Revolutionary War?
- What are the conditions, including the economy, in your country?

Students will read their text and answer the questions. They should also discuss the readings and answers with their partners. Once they understand their materials, they begin to write the script for their poems. Instructions for writing the scripts are:

1. Create a title for your script.

2. Begin the script with a statement that people from both perspectives would make.

3. Next, each student writes five to eight statements showing his or her particular perspective.

4. Then, students combine their statements into a poetic format.

5. Every four or so lines, another common statement should be inserted.

6. Finally, a common statement concludes the script.

Assessment would indicate whether or not students understood the differing viewpoints and used information gleaned from the text.

(This activity was adapted from a presentation by Laura Wakefield at an NCHE Colloquium for teachers in Fairfax County, Virginia.)

Marking and Thinking

Textbooks and other expository text include a great amount of information. So, how can teachers help students distinguish between what is important and what is supporting or interesting material? This is a very challenging skill for students at all levels, and teachers must constantly revisit this topic. Often words such as *important*, *main*, and *first* give students clues about what is most important. However, these signal words are sometimes missing. Marking and Thinking is an interactive way of having students make connections, determine important information, look for information that is interesting, and ask questions if they do not understand. A teacher begins by selecting an appropriate piece of text that can be copied and put on an overhead so the strategy can be modeled. The coding system in Figure 4.2 is also displayed. As the teacher reads the passage aloud, the * marks important information, the ! designates interesting information, and the ? is used when questions arise. When the teacher makes personal connections to the text or connections to material previously covered, the + symbol is used.

Figure 4.2: Coding for Marking and Thinking

+	This reminds me of….
*	Important information
!	Wow! Interesting information
?	I don't understand

Once the strategy is taught, students read a short passage independently. They use the coding system on self-stick notes to mark sentences or phrases in the passage. When students have finished the passage, they are organized into small groups to discuss what they found important, interesting, confusing, or connected to what they already knew. They discuss similarities and differences in their coding and share justifications for their markings. Finally, students are brought together as an entire group to compare what groups found important or interesting. As the passage is discussed, the students should defend their ideas about what is most important and what is simply interesting information. The teacher should also list questions and clarify any misunderstandings. The discussion helps the teacher informally assess learning and guides further instruction.

Making Inferences

In social studies, textbooks and other examples of expository material require students to use skills of analysis and to make inferences. "Inferential thinking occurs when text clues merge with the reader's prior knowledge and questions to point toward a conclusion about the underlying theme or idea in a text" (Harvey & Goudvis, 2000, p. 23). In other words, students use what they know to fill in the gaps when they read informational texts. But as the texts become more difficult, this expectation to make inferences about what they read can become a very challenging task.

Even the youngest children are constantly making inferences in their everyday lives. One way teachers can help with this challenging task is to remind students of these young experiences and show them the parallels in making inferences as they read text. Often, elementary teachers begin by using picture books and asking students to use the words in the text and the visuals to make inferences. To teach this concept at all age levels, teachers must first find out what students already know and then connect that information with new information in the text. When teachers come upon statements in text that lend themselves to making inferences, it is important to model this thinking aloud to show their thought processes. Identify word clues that help make inferences accurate. Students should also discuss words that contribute to their inferences. Examine the following statements to see how simple statements exemplify types of inferences that are often found in social studies readings.

- "When the light in the lighthouse burned out, the darkness was total." What inferences about time can you make? Are there other inferences that can be made?

- "With bellows, a roaring fire, and anvil ready, the apprentice was able to begin the task." What inferences can be made about occupations or pastimes?

- "In the morning, we noticed that the trees were uprooted and homes were missing their rooftops." What cause/effect inferences can you make?

- "The side of his face was swollen, and his tooth ached." What types of problem/solution inferences are possible?

- "While the soldiers marched by, people cheered and had tears in their eyes." What types of feelings and attitudes can you infer?

These are just a few examples of text that require students to make inferences.

It Says . . . I Say . . . and So . . .

It Says . . . I Say . . . and So is a visual scaffold to teach the skill of making inferences. As always, the teacher must model the strategy and revisit it often, thereby providing students with ample opportunities for practice. Begin by providing students with a question about the text that requires some inferential thinking. The key to the entire process is the good question. When teaching the strategy initially, read a passage orally as the students follow along. Then, discuss information in the text that helps answer the question and place that information in the "It Says" column. The teacher could either paraphrase what the text says or quote it directly. Next, verbalize background knowledge and place that in the "I Say" column. The inference, "and So," is made when the students combine what is written in the text with what they think from the "I Say" column.

Figure 4.3 has been completed showing a middle school question that integrates economics and historical information on the California gold rush.

Figure 4.3: It Says . . . I Say . . . and So . . .

Question	It Says	I Say	and So
Read the question.	Find information from the text to help you answer the question.	Consider what you know about the information.	Put together the information from the text with what you know to answer the question.
What can we infer about the lives of the people participating in the California gold rush?	men made money mining women owned boardinghouses men and women ran saloons men used their gold to buy food, clothing, lodging	not all miners struck it rich women did not work in the mine fields	people who provided services had a consistent income

Summarizing

Teachers often say that summarizing is one of the most difficult skills for students to learn. Research supports this (Duke & Pearson, 2002), but becoming skilled at summarizing offers huge benefits. When students can summarize, they recognize the main idea and can eliminate what is unimportant. They are required to think deeply about the information they read and use skills of analysis. They refine their vocabularies, and when they put the main idea into their own words, they also remember the content better. The following strategies can aid students in this skill.

GIST

In this summarizing strategy, middle and high school students need to explain the "gist" of a piece of text by summarizing it in a few words (Moore, Cunningham, & Cunningham, 2006). They look for important information, eliminate unimportant information, remove redundancies, and write a brief summary of 20 words or less. One way to introduce this strategy is to begin by using a short newspaper article with approximately three paragraphs. To help students look for the most important information, they begin by focusing on *who, what, when, where, why,* and *how.* After students have read the article, conduct a class discussion. Ask them to recall the most important information in the text and record this information. Then, have students work as a class to take the important words and condense them into a clear summary of about 20 words. Students will need to think of synonyms and other words that incorporate the meaning of one or two of the words in the initial list. As students become more familiar with the GIST strategy, they can work in pairs and then ultimately independently. With newspaper articles, students also enjoy giving the articles new headlines. This requires them to use the summarized information and condense it even more succinctly.

Magnet Summaries

Magnet summaries (Buehl, 2001) are another good way to teach summarization. Again, students look for the most important information in a reading, eliminate unimportant information, and then write a summary sentence. When a teacher introduces the strategy, using an analogy about a magnet engages student thinking. Just as magnets attract metal objects, so do magnet words attract key information. This strategy works well when using textbooks. Ask each student to read a short section of the textbook on a given topic and look for key words that explain the topic. Lead the students in a class discussion and write the important information about that topic around the word. If the teacher wants students to read about the Serengeti Plain in Africa, a magnet summary might look like Figure 4.4. Discuss the information that students want included on the magnet. Then, model how to write a brief summary sentence using the important words. It is important to help students understand that they might not use all the words, because some are more important than others. The summary statement again should be approximately 20 words in length. As students become more comfortable with the strategy, they may work in small groups or pairs to write magnet summaries for other parts of their textbooks. It is also engaging for students to put their magnet summaries on index cards. The information is on one side of the card, and the sentence summary can be written on the back of the card. When a number of cards are created, they become an excellent study guide for a larger topic.

Figure 4.4: Magnet Summary for the Serengeti Plain

home to great concentration of wildlife

Africa

grassland

acacia bushes/trees

Tanzania   rocky

huge   **Serengeti Plain**

major tourist attraction

forests   animal migrations

A summary sentence for figure 4.4 could be "The vast Serengeti Plain in Tanzania is home to an enormous array of African wildlife and therefore attracts many tourists."

Somebody Wanted But So

Another excellent strategy for summarizing is Somebody Wanted But So (Macon, Bewell, & Vogt, 1991). This strategy is particularly useful when summarizing an event in history. Figure 4.5 provides students with a framework to create their summaries. As always, when teaching the strategy, it is important for the teacher to model it. Begin by reading about an historical event. With the students help, determine who the *Somebody* is and what the somebody *Wanted*. This information is placed in the appropriate columns. What happened to keep them from it is placed in the *But* column and how it all worked out is placed in the *So* column. As students practice using the organizer, they will be able to work in small groups, pairs, or individually to develop summaries. A completed chart for elementary age students on reasons leading to the Revolutionary War is shown in Figure 4.5.

Figure 4.5: Somebody Wanted But So

Somebody	Wanted	But	So
main historical individuals or groups	goals or desires of the group or individuals	the obstacle or conflict created for the individual or group	how the problem was resolved
King George III	*colonists to pay for the French and Indian War*	*The colonists felt taxation without representation was unfair and refused to pay the taxes.*	*The King sent troops to America to try to enforce the laws, thus leading to confrontation.*

Conclusion

There is no getting around it; students in social studies are asked to read a great variety of material but cannot always make meaning from what they read. It is the teacher's responsibility to give them strategies for previewing text and give them a meaningful purpose for reading. It is also important that they are actively engaged as they read. Marking and thinking and paired reading are excellent strategies to foster this engagement. Finally, students must engage in a variety of post-reading strategies. In this chapter, the strategies for making inferences and summarizations are highlighted because these skills are not only challenging but also critically important.

Additional Resources

Beers, K. (2003). *When kids can't read—What teachers can do*. Portsmouth, NH: Heinemann.

Buehl, D. (2001). *Classroom strategies for interactive learning*. Newark Delaware, International Reading Association.

Doty, J. K., Cameron, G. N., & Barton, M. L. (2003). *Teaching reading in social studies: A supplement to teaching reading in the content areas*. Alexandria, VA: Association for Supervision and Curriculum Development.

Macceca, S. (2007). *Reading strategies for social studies*. Huntington Beach, CA: Shell Education.

Robb, L. (2003). *Teaching reading in social studies, science, and math*. New York, NY: Scholastic.

Chapter 4 Reflection

1. What specific reading strategies are most important for your classroom?

_____

_____

_____

_____

2. Currently, how do you explicitly teach reading strategies in your social studies classroom? What works? What does not? Why?

_____

_____

_____

_____

3. Describe at least one strategy for explicitly teaching reading that you will try in the coming months. What text materials will you use?

_____

_____

_____

_____

_____

_____

_____

Strategies for Using Primary Sources

Many years ago, volunteer docents from the National Archives and Research Administration made a classroom outreach visit with facsimiles of primary sources relating to a revolutionary soldier, Simon Fobes. At first, the students were fearful of the resources, which looked daunting to read. However, as teachers helped them analyze the materials and asked probing questions, students became intrigued and came up with their own questions. Suddenly, Simon came alive for them and they had a better understanding of the life of a revolutionary soldier than from any account they could read in their textbook.

This chapter discusses the use of primary sources. Using primary sources adds a "real life element to history" (Vest, 2005, p. 10). Often texts present a dry, fact-filled interpretation of history. However, primary sources can engage students in learning how people during a given time period acted, thought, and felt. The stories of real people make history come alive for students. Students see events from different perspectives, develop historical empathy, see the similarities and differences among people, and make connections to their own lives. Using primary sources helps students develop skills of observation and inquiry. Students ask questions, develop research skills, analyze information, and draw conclusions. They utilize critical thinking skills and learn to think like a historian, geographer, economist, and political scientist.

Exactly what are primary and secondary sources? The Library of Congress defines primary sources as original items or records that have survived from the past, such as clothing, letters, photographs, and manuscripts. They are part of a direct personal experience of a time or event. The Library of Congress states that secondary sources are created by documenting or analyzing someone else's experience to provide a perspective or description of a past event and may have been written shortly after or long after an event took place. Students' textbooks and encyclopedias are secondary sources. It is important for students to realize that not all primary sources and secondary sources are accurate or reliable. Anyone who has created them has a definite point of view or bias. Knowing this creates another layer of analysis for students as they investigate these sources.

This chapter will contain strategies for examining photographs, paintings, written documents, maps, posters, and cartoons. The following chapters will cover the use of oral histories, artifacts, music, and film. A much more detailed book on this topic is *Using Primary Sources in the Classroom* by Kathleen Vest.

Photographs

Students of all ages love looking at photographs, and this is the perfect vehicle to introduce very young children to the concept of primary sources. When they bring photos of themselves as babies and preschoolers, they are beginning to understand that these are their own primary sources. They can also bring pictures of their parents, grandparents, and great-grandparents when they were young children and compare and contrast the photographs. These pictures lead to interesting discussions of change over time. In other photographs, young children can examine changes in clothing, housing, transportation, schooling, work, and leisure activities. Young children delight in comparing their lives with lives of people long ago and can easily complete a two-column data retrieval chart. Figure 5.1 graphically depicts a way to compare a student's own life and the life of a fictional character from a different time period.

Figure 5.1: Comparing Now and Long Ago

	Now	Long Ago
Food		
Clothing		
Housing		
Activities		

As young learners examine other types of photographs, the following graphic organizer, Figure 5.2, is a simple way to focus their thinking.

Figure 5.2: Picture Study

PICTURE STUDY		
Describe the people	**Describe the things**	**Describe the actions**
What do you think about this picture? I think . . .		
I wonder . . .		
A good title for this picture is . . .		

More sophisticated questions for older students include:

- What things in the photograph are familiar to you?
- When was this photograph taken? (time period, season)
- Why was this photograph taken?
- What is the point of view of the photographer?
- How does the photograph make you feel?
- Why is this photograph historically significant?
- What can you infer from this photograph?
- If this person could speak, what do you think he or she would say?
- What other questions do you have?
- How could you find the answers to your questions?

Paintings

Often primary teachers are hesitant to use primary sources because they immediately think that their students cannot read difficult text. However, many primary sources are appealing and easily accessible to very young children. All kindergarten children learn about George Washington. They read a variety of books, some of which have cartoon-like drawings of Washington. Other trade books have combinations of drawings and photographs of primary sources. But why not choose a famous painting that is rich in detail and information? Examine the painting of George Washington's family by Edward Savage (Image 5.1). This painting depicts Washington, his wife and two Custis grandchildren seated at a table looking at a map, a plan for the Federal City. Washington's slave, William Lee, stands in the background.

Image 5.1: *The Washington Family* by Edward Savage

Source: The Granger Collection, New York

Introduce the lesson by asking students where they see images of George Washington. Students will talk about the books in the classroom, but they should also realize that he is on the dollar bill and on coins. Tell them that they can learn a lot about what was important to George Washington by looking at this famous painting. Begin the lesson by asking students what they see in the picture. Then, they can begin making assumptions while answering more probing types of questions, such as:

- Who do you think all the people in the painting are?

- What kind of clothes are they wearing? Why is George Washington wearing a uniform?

- Is the family rich or poor? How do you know?

- Why do you think there's a map and globe in the picture?

- Who do you think the man in the back of the picture is?

- How is this picture similar or different from a picture of your family?

- What questions do you still have?

- Where could we find the answers to your questions?

The discussion that concludes the investigation of the portrait can lead students to investigate Washington's life in greater depth.

Another excellent painting for this type of activity is the *George Washington* (Lansdowne portrait) by Gilbert Stuart (Image 5.2). This painting is one of the most famous of Washington and the objects included in the portrait are symbolic of what Washington viewed as his important legacy. Students from upper elementary through high school can use investigative and analytic skills as they study this painting.

Image 5.2: *George Washington* **by Gilbert Stuart**

Source: The Library of Congress

Then, have students compare it to the painting below of Washington as the commander in the Revolutionary War.

Image 5.3: *George Washington* **by Charles W. Peale**

Source: The Library of Congress

- How are these two paintings different?
- How are they alike?
- What would Washington say as a young man?
- How would this change as he grew older?

Written Documents

As students get older, they are more capable of analyzing written documents. These include but are certainly not limited to diaries, wills, paper money, census records, newspapers, and letters. When using a written document, it is important to choose it very carefully in order to ensure that the document meets your objectives. Consider the length of the document, its style and difficulty, and the capabilities of the students. Students enjoy seeing a copy of the original document and should be asked to spend some time deciphering it. However, depending on the document and abilities of the students, a typed copy of the text may be provided. If the document is lengthy, only the essential excerpt(s) should be used. Also, before having students tackle the document, teachers must teach any challenging vocabulary and ensure that students have the necessary background knowledge. Generic questions that can be used with most documents include:

- What type of written document is this?
- Who wrote it and when was it written?
- Who is the audience for the document?
- What is the purpose of the document?
- What three things did the author write that you think are important?
- What can you learn about life at the time the document was written?
- What unanswered questions do you still have?

Questions are adapted from The National Archives and Records Administration's Document Analysis Worksheets.

Diaries, letters, and journals are very engaging and can transmit a vast amount of information about life in the past. It is particularly refreshing for students to look at the past through the eyes of other children and young adults whose stories do not typically appear in textbooks and other informational sources. An excellent source for diaries and journals covering the scope of American history is *America's History Through Young Voices* edited by Richard M. Wyman (2005). In this book, there are entries from the "Journal of Sallie Hester" describing life on the Overland Trail. The application questions below correspond to the historical thinking processes. They can be used for students' journal entries and then shared in small group or classroom discussions.

- Chronological Thinking—Cite specific diary entries to show the change in Hester's attitude toward the overland crossing over the course of her journey.

- Historical Comprehension—Write a letter from Hester's perspective to a schoolmate back in Indiana describing the overland crossing.

- Historical Analysis and Interpretation—Analyze whether the history of the United States would have changed had gold not been discovered in California.

- Historical Issues-Analysis and Decision-Making—Analyze the impact of the overland migration on the indigenous people with whom the emigrants came into contact.

These statements were shared by Dr. Ted. D. R. Green, Webster University.

The following letter (Figure 5.3) to President Dwight Eisenhower is written by a child. Michael Rosenberg had previously written the president asking that he let his parents out of prison. His parents are the famous

Julius and Ethel Rosenberg. He obviously hopes to make a personal plea to the President. This very personal note from a child pulls on the heartstrings of all as his parents are headed toward execution. For a moment, even those who believe the Rosenbergs are guilty realize these are real people with young children who desperately want them home.

Figure 5.3: Letter to President Eisenhower

1953 June 17 P.M. 12:50
The President
The White House

Today 4 o'clock Robby, my grandmother, and I are going to Washington. Since you have not answered my letters yet I would like to speak to you and tell you how good my mommy and daddy are. If you are busy please give a letter to the policeman whom I gave a letter to on Sunday so he can give it to me.

Very Truly Yours,
Michael Rosenberg

Source: Dwight D. Eisenhower Presidential Library

Consider the following journal (Figure 5.4) written by Christopher Columbus. While this journal is not written by a child, it is written by someone familiar to students.

Figure 5.4: Journal of Columbus

Sunday, September 9, 1492
This day we completely lost sight of land. Many men sighed and wept for fear they would not see it again for a long time. I comforted them with great promises of lands and riches. I decided to count fewer miles than we actually made. I did this so the sailors would not think themselves as far from Spain as they really were. For myself I kept a confidential accurate reckoning. Tonight I made ninety miles.

Have students close their eyes and imagine they found this journal on the ship. Would they read it? Would they tell the other sailors about it? Why or why not?

Signage

Signage includes all documents categorized as posters, advertisements, and notices. These documents are often good ways for students to begin using primary sources. The text varies in length and sometimes a picture or illustration is added. The document questions listed on pages 78–79 can be easily used for these documents. Additionally, the teacher should ask:

- Who was the intended audience?
- What symbols are used and are they clear?
- What action does the author hope that the audience will take after viewing the poster?

Image 5.4: *Auction Broadside, 1829*

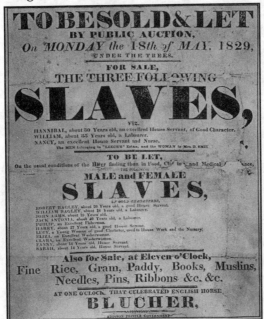

Source: The Granger Collection, New York

The signage (Image 5.4) helps students to make the connection that slaves were real people. By this time in history, slaves had Americanized names and many of them were young. The signage also shows students that this auction would take place where people could buy food and sewing supplies. If the people waited around until the afternoon, they could even be entertained by a famous horse show. This document gives a very clear picture of the attitudes toward slaves at that time.

Middle school and high school students studying World Wars I and II enjoy examining the propaganda posters (Image 5.5) created by the United States government.

Image 5.5: *Propaganda Posters*

Source: The Library of Congress

Students can be put in the position of designers as they think of ways to improve these advertisements. They can compare and contrast these war posters with one another and other wars including World War II, Vietnam, and the Cold War. How have they changed over time? Other ways to integrate art produced by the government will be discussed in Chapter 8.

Image 5.6: *Thomas Jefferson Advertisement*

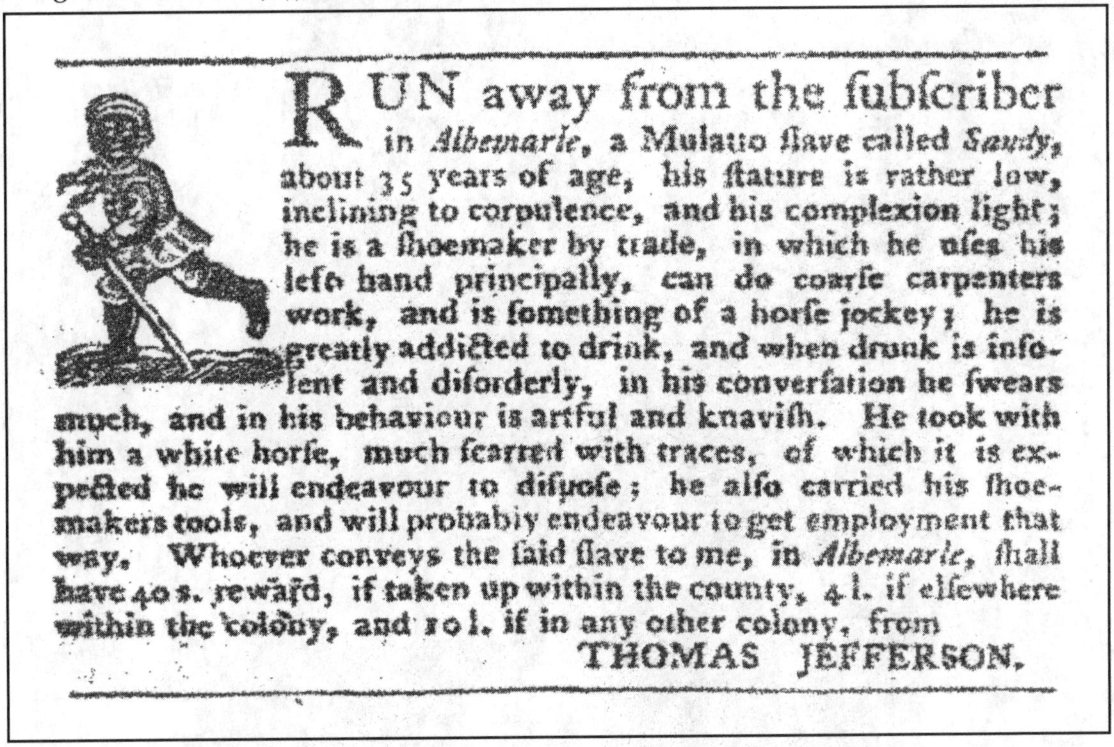

RUN away from the ſubſcriber in *Albemarle*, a Mulatto ſlave called *Sandy*, about 35 years of age, his ſtature is rather low, inclining to corpulence, and his complexion light; he is a ſhoemaker by trade, in which he uſes his left hand principally, can do coarſe carpenters work, and is ſomething of a horſe jockey; he is greatly addicted to drink, and when drunk is inſolent and diſorderly, in his converſation he ſwears much, and in his behaviour is artful and knaviſh. He took with him a white horſe, much ſcarred with traces, of which it is expected he will endeavour to diſpoſe; he alſo carried his ſhoemakers tools, and will probably endeavour to get employment that way. Whoever conveys the ſaid ſlave to me, in *Albemarle*, ſhall have 40 s. reward, if taken up within the county, 4 l. if elſewhere within the colony, and 10 l. if in any other colony, from

THOMAS JEFFERSON.

Show students the advertisement above (Image 5.6). Cover the bottom of this advertisement so that students cannot see that Thomas Jefferson wrote this ad. Based on the ad, have students create character sketches of the person who wrote this. Then, reveal the true author. This will make an impression that students will not soon forget.

Maps

Using a variety of maps can help students practice applying map-reading skills and learn the skills of a geographer or cartographer.

Image 5.7: *John Smith's Map of Virginia*

Source: Historical Documents Co.

This map (Image 5.7) has many artistic details to analyze. Give students magnifying glasses, divide the map into quarters, and let groups analyze a section. Some students will notice that there are sea monsters in the waters. They will see the detailed drawing in the top left corner. Students will wonder what these symbols mean. Sample questions to ask include:

- What is the title of the map?

- When was the map created?

- What type of map is it?

- Why was the map created?

- What is the scale of the map?

- What is its orientation?

- Does it have a map key? What do the symbols represent?

- Does it have additional inscriptions or artistic features? Describe them.

- Who would use this map?

- If it is an historic map, is it still accurate today?

- How does it help you understand the period you are studying?

- What additional questions do you have?

Students love to examine the 1810 map that William Clark made after the Lewis and Clark exploration of the Louisiana Purchase. If possible, introduce the map by providing students with magnifying glasses and ask them to scan the map, make predictions about its purpose, and note interesting features. Then, have students answer the questions above to begin analyzing the map. Provide students with a contemporary map of Lewis and Clark's route and have them complete graphic organizers, such as Venn diagrams, to compare and contrast the two maps.

Image 5.8: *Map of Dachau*

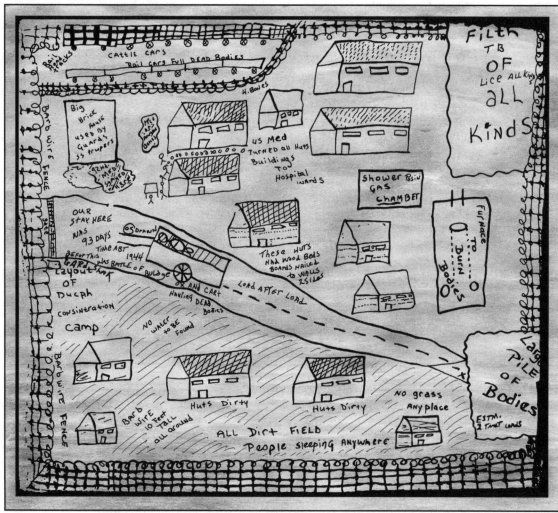

At a first glance, students will think a child created this map (Image 5.8). Begin with predictions. Who made this map? How do we know he or she was not a professional cartographer? Why would he or she draw a map like this? They will be surprised to know that a medical army officer, who helped liberate prisoners at Dachau, drew it in 1945.

Image 5.9: *The Battle of Bunker Hill*

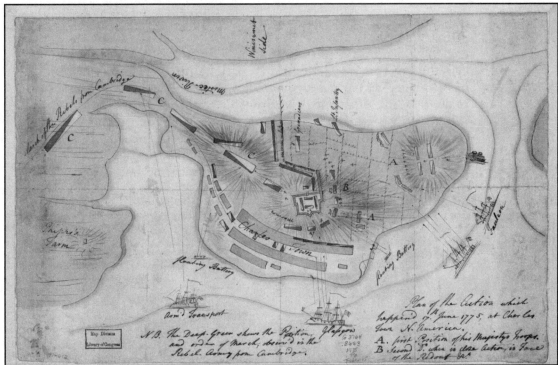

Source: The Library of Congress

This map of Bunker Hill, correctly named Breed's Hill (Image 5.9), shows the three hills on the peninsula of Charlestown. It was the site of a battle during the American Revolution. Ask students to come up with an offensive battle plan if they were to attack the peninsula or a defensive battle plan if they were to defend the peninsula. Then show the students the movement of both the American troops and the British troops. They can compare their ideas with what really happened there.

Cartoons

Political cartoons are among the most challenging of primary sources for students because they need a great deal of background information and the cartoons have symbolism that students find challenging. Cartoons have a very specific point of view and are created to make a point, influence opinion, persuade, or ridicule. When choosing cartoons, a teacher must consider what students need to know before understanding the message of the cartoon. If students are studying the causes of the American Revolution, they can view the cartoon below.

Image 5.10: *The Repeal, or Funeral Procession, of the Stamp Act*

Source: The Library of Congress

The following questions will focus the analysis of the cartoon. In this case, they range from the most basic questions to more challenging questions. Upper-elementary students can begin to evaluate political cartoons, but they are used more frequently as students move from middle school to high school.

- What is the title or caption of the cartoon?

- What people and objects are in the cartoon?

- What words are in the cartoon?

- What are the symbols and what do they mean?

- Explain any exaggerations in the cartoon.

- What is the point of view of the cartoon?

- What is difficult to understand about the cartoon? Why?

- Who would agree with the point of view in the cartoon? Who would disagree?

- What are the cartoonist's political views?

The cartoon on the following page (Image 5.11) at first glance looks simple. But there are many hidden meanings that even older students may not understand without some guidance. Look at the way these two adults are dressed. What time is it? What does that matter? Why are the babies crying? Notice the cat's behavior. Is this cartoon for or against women's suffrage? Female students might say it is for women's suffrage. Male students might say that it is against women's suffrage. Point out that this is a good example of different viewpoints and backgrounds.

Image 5.11: *Election Day*

Source: *The Library of Congress*

From Document to Thesis

When middle school and high school students are able to analyze a variety of sources, they write as historians. Consider a project in which students study primary sources from World War II and prepare to write articles about D-Day. From initial questions, they conduct historical inquiries to transform the questions into thesis statements that direct their writings.

Initially, the teacher collects a variety of primary sources including photographs, maps, government documents, speeches, letters, and maps. Students begin by writing questions to direct their inquiries. Figure 5.5 lists some of the primary sources that might be collected and their sources for teachers. Students read each, determine the point of view, and make notes for themselves.

Figure 5.5: Documents for D-Day Project

Document	Source and Brief Description
Eisenhower Addressing the Troops, June 5, 1944	Photograph: National Archives and Records Administration (NARA), ARC identifier 531217
Eisenhower's Order of the Day (just before D-Day)	Motivational letter to forces: "Eisenhower Speaks" Lesson Plan (The draft of the letter with handwritten changes by Eisenhower can also be found at the Eisenhower Library.)
First Report after D-Day Begins, June 6, 1944	SHAEF message from Eisenhower to Marshall: Eisenhower Library, Digital Documents Project in Research section
Eisenhower's D-Day Failure Message, June 5, 1944	Handwritten note in case the invasion failed: "Eisenhower Speaks" Lesson Plan found at National World War II Museum website
Operation Overlord Map	Map showing attack: available in a variety of places, often found in textbooks
Minute by Minute Progression of D-Day Events	From 00:15 through the day: found under "World War II History"
D-Day by the Numbers	Numbers of soldiers, nationalities of combatants, and casualties: www.nationalww2museum.org/education/lessonplans.html
The Diary of Lieutenant Sidney J. Montz	Short diary entries from May through July, 1944: "A Turning Point in WWII": www.nationalww2museum.org/education/lessonplans.html

When students have read the sources, they will pick three of them and describe how they differ in terms of purpose or points of view. They then use examples from the documents to discuss the difference between facts and opinions or interpretation. They also look for bias in the documents. Finally, students identify those documents they consider most reliable and discuss the criteria they used for making those decisions. When students have completed their analyses, they return to their initial questions and craft thesis statements that direct their inquiries. They pick two or three of the resources that support their theses, take notes on their reasoning, and use the information to write their articles about D-Day. Because of the diversity of documents, this lesson is an excellent example of how teachers can differentiate to meet the needs of diverse learners. It also integrates reading, writing, and critical thinking skills.

Conclusion

Primary sources bring the social studies alive for students. Through photographs, artwork, artifacts, maps, cartoons, and a wealth of written documents, students see events from different perspectives, develop empathy, and make connections. The documents challenge students to develop analysis skills and probe deeper into the real stories of people. When chosen carefully, they greatly enhance the study of the content areas.

Additional Resources

American Memory	http://www.memory.loc.gov/ammem
Colonial Williamsburg	http://www.history.org
Eisenhower Library	http://www.eisenhower.utexas.edu/
Learning Page for Teachers	http://memory.loc.gov/learn
Lewis and Clark Expedition	http://www.loc.gov/exhibits/lewisandclark/
The Library of Congress	http://www.loc.gov
The National Archives and Records Administration	http://www.archives.gov
National World War II Museum	http://www.nationalww2museum.org
Primary Source Analysis Worksheets	http://www.archives.gov/education/lessons/worksheets/index.html
Resources for Teaching American History	http://www.smithsoniansource.org
Smithsonian Education	http://www.smithsonianeducation.org/
Teaching with Primary Sources	http://www.primarysourcelearning.org

Chapter 5 Reflection

1. When teaching the difference between primary and secondary sources, certain sources fall into a gray area. How can you help students understand the difference between primary and secondary sources?

   _____

   _____

   _____

   _____

2. Consider a unit that you will teach soon. How can you incorporate more primary sources?

   _____

   _____

   _____

   _____

   _____

3. What challenges do you expect? How will you address them?

   _____

   _____

   _____

   _____

   _____

   _____

   _____

Engaging Students in Research

Why do social scientists do research? Simply, they want answers to questions they encounter when reading or thinking about their discipline. Why did Abraham Lincoln free the slaves only in the Southern states that had left the union? What would happen if electoral votes could be apportioned according to the popular vote in each state?

Why should students do research? When students construct their own knowledge and answer questions that they find interesting, it always results in a final product that conveys their own thinking rather than a repetition of others. One of the primary joys in learning is sharing that knowledge with someone else, particularly if it is something the student finds fascinating, engaging, and relevant. What does research say about the benefits of students constructing their own learning? The converging research outlined in *Igniting Student Potential* (Gunn, Richburg, & Smilkstein, 2007, p. 61), concludes, "These various views all explain that learning starts with what the learner already knows, that new knowledge must be connected to it and then constructed through experiencing and processing, stage upon stage, neural structure upon neural structure, to higher and more complex levels of knowledge, skill, and understanding."

One of the greatest frustrations that teachers report is the result of the research their students are doing. The typical history report boils down to "born-did-died." While the teacher finds grading such a paper as dull drudgework, imagine the student trying to write a research paper that is little more than a recitation of chronological facts.

Robert Bain (2007) noted that historians start with a question and teachers tend to start with the answer, the effects of which puts the teacher in the center of learning and not the student. Therein lies the crux of the problem of how to get students to write and think in a nontraditional manner to construct their own knowledge.

While it may seem that asking primary and intermediate elementary students to construct their own knowledge is beyond their cognitive abilities, experience says that it is not. The caveat is that it must be taught or scaffolded in such a way that allows students at the various levels to practice constructing knowledge at appropriate cognitive levels.

When studying American history, second or third grade students are usually asked to answer the "who, what, when, and where" questions. These are important guidelines for students at that level for understanding the basic facts about historical people and events. The critical question is really "so what?" or "why is this important to learn?" or "what's the significance?" Students who are taught to think about and respond to these questions are better able to apply those skills with greater depth throughout their K–12 experiences.

Clearly, it is necessary to first model the kind of thinking required to answer these higher level questions, but equally important is developing or using a set of prompts that require students to analyze and synthesize the facts they have learned. Examples of the kinds of prompts that might be used are:

- Why is it important for us to learn about_____? (event)
- Why do we celebrate_____? (holiday)
- Why do we remember _____? (notable person)
- What is it that the person did that makes him or her notable?
- Why does this symbol represent _____? (flag, monument, etc.)
- Why is this important in our lives today?

Student responses should:

- be historically relevant;
- contain historical details applicable to the topic;
- use appropriate vocabulary specific to the topic;
- capture the historical significance (essence) of the topic being studied.

How to Generate Questions for Research

Research questions can arise in a variety of ways. As noted earlier, the historian looks for answers—starts with a question or a problem. Sometimes that question emerges from a natural curiosity about an event or some research being undertaken for another purpose. Other times the question arises from confusion about conflicting sources. Students do not perform historical investigations just because they are confused about events. They investigate because there are contradictions found in the available information about the event or topic. (Marzano, Pickering, & Pollock, 2001). As students investigate history, they will realize there are no quick answers.

Other sources for generating questions for historical research are images and artifacts. When asked how she approaches a heretofore-unseen image, historian Jennifer Keene (2006) replied, "I start reading." She researches the background of the image, also known as *metadata* (when produced, by whom, where, etc.). Her goal is to contextualize the image so that when she studies it more closely she understands as much as possible about why and how it came into being. For students who live in a world of images, beginning research with something visual or tactile "hooks" students and gets them started asking questions that use the full range of Bloom's continuum of thinking skills.

Writing Assignment Model

An excellent strategy for helping middle school and high school students construct their own learning and write about it can be found in the Fall 1991 OAH Magazine of History. Professors Kline Capps and David E. Vocke (1991) discuss ways to develop higher-level thinking skills through American history writing assignments. In the article, the authors identify a process the teacher can use to guide students in approaching the ubiquitous writing assignment that results in papers that mirror their thinking and uses facts to bolster their arguments rather than a list of events or people who were born-did-died. Figure 6.1 is a summary of Capps and Vocke's process adapted to a linear format that is easy for both teachers and students to understand and use effectively. Throughout the process, students should record their learning in a manner that is easily retrievable and mean-ingful to them—should it be graphic organizers, notes, or some other form.

It is important to remember, however, that as with any new skill the process to master it must be taught, retaught, and explicitly revisited during the school year. The first few times this process is used, the teacher should plan to walk students through each step. As students become more comfortable with this kind of divergent thinking, they will be able to become more independent as they continue to use the process.

Figure 6.1: Writing Assignment Model

- Activate or capitalize on students' prior knowledge.
  - Elicit current perceptions of an historical figure or event.
  - Discuss and record words or phrases that could be categorized.
- Categorize the information as a class and record it on the board or chart paper.
- Introduce conflicting characterizations or accounts that would stimulate students to ponder the reasons for the divergent information. Use film clips, primary-source documents, secondary sources, etc.
- Students work in small groups to categorize and describe the differing information.
  - Help students generate questions to extend their knowledge to validate one perspective or point of view.
- Provide students with additional conflicting information designed to create more conversation or questions about the true nature of the person or event.
- Ask students to share their versions of the "truth" by providing them the opportunity to examine the viewpoints of others and how they interpret the information provided.
- Ask students to express their knowledge by writing responses to a question (generated by either the teacher or student) that elicits higher-level or critical thinking.

Turning Students into Historians

Teachers can use the information in the previous chapter on primary sources to facilitate students' thinking, researching, and writing as historians. Primary sources are rich with information and naturally expose students to how things change over time, multiple perspectives, and themes or ideas over time.

Photographs of the same location taken a number of years apart provide students the opportunity to look at how the environment or a landscape has changed. Similarly, photos of such things as farming implements, machines, or forms of transportation can illustrate the impact of science and technology on society. A collection of several pairs of photos about similar topics or areas can be used to have students reflect on larger questions about changes in a region, etc. A series of questions about each pair of photos is helpful to guide students in their analysis and understanding of the historical context (Eastman, 1995).

A collection of primary sources (documents, testimony, maps, or letters) about a particular event offers students opportunities to practice the skills employed by historians as they write about the past. Events that have an element of controversy or contain contradictory information tend to be more engaging such as Lexington Green—April 1775 or Sand Creek, Colorado—November 1864 (Zola, 1996). An excellent way to illustrate to students the concept of multiple perspectives through photographs is to show them photos taken by Mathew Brady during the Civil War. These photos often provide interesting perspectives. The photographs of Antietam, in particular, record opposing perspectives of the battlefield. Taken in opposite directions, one reflects the bucolic beauty and serenity of the area. The second, taken at the same time in the opposite direction, shows victims of the battle lying helter-skelter where they fell.

A collection of primary sources illustrating different aspects of a common theme allows students to grapple with issues larger than the actual events and understand that, often, different generations are faced with the same concerns and dilemmas. For example, there are themes or ideas that can be investigated over time such as war, reform, disease, and a local city or state. A list of events from specific time periods that relate to a theme such as "The United States in War" could include events from the War of 1812, Civil War, Spanish-American War, the world wars, Korea, Vietnam, and Iraq. Similarly, students could investigate different topics related to the same "The United States in War" theme. Those categories or topics might include the role of African Americans in wars, what United States leaders said, the role of newspapers, or opponents' points of view (Kobrin, 1996).

It is not enough for students to merely conduct their research. The facts that they are gathering only become useful if they can be organized into an easily accessible and usable form. There is a range of social studies writing strategies that include a variety of graphic organizers that can be found in *Writing Strategies for Social Studies* by Sarah Kartchner Clark. The strategies and graphic organizers are applicable to students K–12 but require adaptation for students' cognitive abilities.

Figure 6.2 illustrates a type of information organizer students might use to find differences and commonalities in a set of documents as they begin a study of life in a Japanese American internment camp.

Figure 6.2: Historical Data Analysis Guide

Japanese American Incarceration at Amache Camp Primary Sources	What type of primary source is this?	What was the purpose of the primary source?	When was the primary source produced?	What information can be gleaned from the primary source?
Amache High School student letters				
Photos of the barracks at Amache Camp				
Executive Order 9066				

Beyond the Report

Constructing knowledge by doing research is engaging for students, but a key to the process is having a product that is significant, interesting, useful, and relevant. Students should understand the purpose for their research at the start of any project and how they will be expected to demonstrate and use their learning. Several examples of products for student research are: debates, mock trials, simulations, role-playing, museum exhibits, presentations such as National History Day, or submissions to a journal such as the Concord Review. For additional ideas, see the list of project assessments on page 163 in Chapter 10.

Students "Doing" Oral History

For students of all ages, "doing" oral history presents unique and meaningful opportunities to conduct historical research. For younger students, it can begin with an interview of grandparents, parents, or others in their communities. The research conducted by middle school and high school students in more formal oral-history projects may have the potential to be used by other historians in a citation or to be published. Learning history by doing history is an effective and relevant way to get students involved in constructing their own learning.

The oral historian never undertakes an interview without having thoroughly researched his or her subject. The key to a successful oral-history interview is a deep understanding of the context into which the subject's life fits. This depth of knowledge serves two very important purposes. First, it enables the interviewer to prepare substantive questions designed to elicit reflective and thoughtful responses from the subject of the history. Second, it allows the interviewer to ask "on the spot" follow-up questions that both probe and challenge the interviewee to remember in greater detail. A well-researched interviewer can offer information that clarifies the responses of the interviewee.

Good questions make for great answers. In the case of doing oral history, good questions are a prerequisite to an interview that will serve as a valuable primary source for study now and in the future. Understanding how to develop open-ended questions and the ability to use follow-up questions that clarify and elucidate are important skills for students doing oral history and beyond.

Examples of open-ended questions for oral history are:

- Who is the person who had the greatest impact on your life?

- What leader do you admire the most and why?

- What are some of the most difficult choices you've had to make and what made them difficult?

- What do you hope to leave behind after you are gone?

Numerous print resources exist that delineate the steps for teachers to plan, organize, implement, and manage oral-history projects. Two sources are *The Oral History Manual* by Barbara W. Sommer and Mary Kay Quinlan and the Spring 1997 issue of the *OAH Magazine of History*. Online resources are abundant as well. Each state has at least one oral-history organization. There are also regional organizations that fall under the auspices of the American Association for State and Local History (AASLH). The Library of Congress's Oral History Project is viewable online and helps teachers find out how to involve students in doing oral history.

Service Learning vs. Community Service

Perhaps the most common problem-based learning is service learning. Many schools nationwide have made service learning a part of their graduation requirements for students. It is important, however, to differentiate service learning from community service.

- Service learning focuses on students learning a process for activism in the community that requires a great deal of research and knowledge about the issue or topic under study in the classroom.

- Community service focuses on involvement in the community through volunteerism and is often extraneous to the curriculum being taught during the school day.

Both types of community involvement have purpose, value, and a place for use for students, but service learning, in particular, is an excellent model to engage students in problem-based learning. There are two out-standing models for teaching the processes of service learning that are solid, well-researched, and documented in terms of their success in changing student attitudes toward civic involvement as well as deeply immersing them in a study of a current school, community, or state issue. Both of these programs are geared toward upper-elementary, middle, and high school students.

Active Citizenship Today [ACT]

Active Citizenship Today of the Constitutional Rights Foundation is recommended for the middle school and high school levels. Written in an accessible manner for students, it outlines a process for identifying an issue or concern to the community and taking action. The five-step process includes:

- Where Do You Live? Looking at Your Community
- What's the Problem? Focusing on an Issue
- Who's Doing What? Searching for Solutions
- What Can You Do? Exploring Options
- What Will You Do? Taking Action

We the People: Project Citizen [PC]

The Project Citizen (PC) program is developed by the Center for Civic Education and has in many ways a similar framework to that of ACT's. It teaches students a process for researching the public policy related to an issue and asks them to offer an alternative solution to the problem. The difference in the two programs is that PC culminates with students participating in a competition where they present their issues and solutions to a group of adult judges, one of whom is an expert in a field related to the chosen topic, with the option of taking action.

The PC process includes:

- Introduction to public policy
- Identifying problems to be dealt with by public policy

- Selecting a problem(s) for your class to study
- Gathering information on the problem you will study
- Organizing the information you have gathered
- Developing a portfolio to present your research
- Presenting your portfolio in a simulated public hearing
- Reflecting on your experience
- Why is citizen participation important to democracy?

Case Studies

Case studies are one of the most effective problem-based strategies. Case studies pose a problem from history for students to discuss and solve. A key part of the case study is the inclusion of primary-source material. The teacher prepares the case study for students and distributes copies of the problem as well as the supporting primary-source material. The following steps are most helpful in creating case studies for your students.

Step 1: Clarify objectives—What does the teacher want students to learn from the discussion of the case? What do they know already that applies to the case? What are the issues (central and peripheral) that may be raised in discussion? Can the case "carry" the discussion? Is it appropriate to your objectives?

Step 2: Plan and prepare—How will the case and discussion be introduced? What preparation is required for students? (Written summaries and reaction papers? Analyses and discussion skills?) What question(s) will open the discussion? How will class time be appropriated for the issues to be discussed? Which concepts will be applied or extracted from the discussion? How will the discussion be concluded? How will students evaluate their own participation in the discussion? How will the teacher evaluate the participants?

Step 3: Consider what's going on—Who are the historical actors and what are their perspectives? What are the relationships among the actors? What is the chronology of events? What, in particular, is the perspective of the protagonist, the decision maker?

Step 4: Analysis of the case—What is the central problem, the decision to be made? What are the issues? What theories, or concepts are applicable to the situation presented?

Step 5: Actions to be taken—What is the variety of possible solutions to the problem presented? How will historical evidence and conceptual support for the proposed solutions be used? How will the proposed solutions be evaluated in light of their historical context? Is there an alternative, a "Plan B," just in case there is a need for one?

Step 6: Evaluation—How will the content knowledge of the case, the contribution of each student to the discussion and group work, and the historical relevance and quality of the solution presented be evaluated?

The Boston Tea Party can be an example of a case study. In planning and preparing for this case study, a teacher would want to include the economic, political, and social issues that existed prior to the event. As the teacher summarizes the information for the case study, he or she needs to be sure to balance the information given to students presenting both the British and colonial points of view. Including excerpts from written documents, images, and charts adds to your ability to present an engaging, well-rounded portrayal of the case. The teacher will also want to cite the sources used, both primary and secondary, including page numbers for students who may wish to further investigate the case.

Tadahisa Kuroda, History Professor Emeritus from Skidmore College, has perfected the use of case studies. He recommends that students be given the case-study packet prior to the discussion in class and come prepared with a one-to-two-page summary of the points they wish to make regarding the case study. When the case study is completed, Dr. Kuroda has a variety of assessment questions he asks of his students. Among them are: What is the most important thing you learned from other students? What is the most important thing you offered to other students? How did the content from the case study apply to either what is being studied in class or to your own life? These questions encourage students to value the thinking of their classmates and appreciate what can be learned from others.

Case studies can be produced by the teacher from scratch or adapted from other sources. Three sources in particular that lend themselves to this kind of adaptation are *After the Fact: The Art of Historical Detection* by Davidson and Lytle, *American Experiences* by Roberts and Olson, and *Teaching U.S. History as Mystery* by Gerwin and Zevin. A number of sources are also available that present both sides of an issue that are helpful in designing a case-study exercise.

Conclusion

Student research and project-based learning provide unique opportunities for teachers to engage their students in learning the concepts that make up social studies. There is an abundance of research to support the importance of student involvement, authentic experience, and relevance. More than any other curriculum content area, social studies have the potential to offer students this kind of learning. While planning for and implementing this kind of learning require a great deal of time upfront on the part of the teacher, the benefits far outweigh the time it takes to plan. During implementation of a research- or project-based activity, the teacher will act as the "guide on the side" rather than the "sage on the stage." Students learn more effectively when they are constructing their own knowledge, and student research- and project-based assignments provide students these opportunities.

Additional Resources

Davidson, J. W., & Lytle, M. H. (2000). *After the fact: The art of historical detection.* Boston: McGraw Hill.

Gerwin, D., & Zevin, J. (2003). *Teaching U.S. history as mystery.* Portsmouth, NH: Heinemann.

Roberts, R., & Olson, J. S. (1994). *American experiences: Readings in American history.* New York: Harper Collins.

Chapter 6 Reflection

1. Think about a research project you have had your students undertake in your classroom. How might you adapt it to elicit higher levels of thinking?

   _____

   _____

   _____

   _____

2. How might you incorporate more time for student research in your already overloaded curriculum?

   _____

   _____

   _____

   _____

   _____

3. Which of the ideas discussed in this chapter will you implement in your teaching? What content will you use? What challenges might you face?

   _____

   _____

   _____

   _____

   _____

   _____

   _____

Hands-on Strategies and Simulations

When adults or high school students are asked, "What do you remember most about your social studies classrooms in elementary school or middle school?" often the reply describes a hands-on activity, interactive simulation, or culminating unit activity. These experiences become part of the lasting memories of students. These were the experiences that engaged them and information from these experiences remain with students for a long time.

Students must participate actively in studying social studies and be engaged in authentic and purposeful activities. "Research is now validating what teachers have known intuitively all along: hands-on learning increases retention and understanding" (Sundem & Pikiewicz, 2005, p. 4). Students need multiple opportunities to touch objects, generate curiosity, and learn to make inferences. They need to participate in simulations or role-plays that enable them to feel like they've participated in an historical event. They look at events from different perspectives so they can understand the motives of individuals and the reasons for their choices. Simulations give students opportunities to experience some of the feelings and issues confronting historical figures. This chapter examines a number of hands-on strategies as well as simulations.

Objects Tell Stories

Objects tell about the everyday life of a culture and make history tangible. Using a very familiar object, such as a cup from a fast-food restaurant, is a quick and easy way to engage students in learning from objects. Divide the students into cooperative learning groups and have them pretend to be archaeologists 2,000 years from now. Give each group a soda cup and ask them: "If you uncovered this cup, what would you learn about the society that made and used the object?" Have students first describe what they see (form, material, pattern, words, colors). Then ask, "What do you think it was made of? Who made it? Who might have used it? How was it used? What do you notice about the designs or motifs? What can we learn about the time period in which it was made?"

Once the teacher has discussed this everyday object, he or she can introduce an object related to the unit under study. In this case, a teacher might use an actual object, a replica, or a picture of an object. Use Chart 7.1 to guide questioning. An *Artifact Analysis Worksheet* can also be obtained from the National Archives and Records Administration website (www.archives.gov/index.html). Search using the words, *artifact analysis worksheet*.

Chart 7.1: Studying Artifacts

Studying Artifacts

- What do you think it is made of (e.g., bone, pottery, wood, metal, leather, plastic)?
- How does it look and feel (e.g., shape, color, texture, weight, any print)?
- What do you think it was used for?
- Who might have used it?
- Who do you think made it?
- What do you notice about the designs (or motifs)?
- Are there any interesting words or phrases on the artifact? In what language?
- What can we learn about the people who made or used this object?
- Were the people rich or poor? Why do you think that?
- Is the object really old? Or was it made recently? Why do you think that?
- Is this a one-of-a-kind artifact or are there many just like it?
- What can we learn about the time period in which it was made?
- What object do we have today that is similar to this object?

Teachers often ask how to get objects for use in their classrooms. When teachers have students study now and long ago, excellent sources for objects are flea markets and antique stores. Museums or living history sites also have replicas of objects for students. *Colonial Williamsburg,* for instance, has an array of toys, children's games and colonial money. Through their catalogue, teachers may purchase artifact "kits" such as items in a slave's bag or woman's pocket. *Colonial Williamsburg* also sells a simulation kit entitled, *Discovering the Past Through Archaeology* which contains reproductions of artifacts, primary documents and instructions for creating an excavation site in the classroom. Check with your local museums and historical sites because some loan historical artifact boxes and trunks for a nominal fee.

If actual artifacts are unavailable, postcards and pictures of objects can also be used. On a trip to Mount Vernon, a class discovered a postcard showing George Washington's fan chair. As students tried to answer some of the questions in Chart 7.1, they also made inferences on why this chair was important to George Washington.

As discussed in Chapter 5 on using primary sources, students enjoy bringing in pictures of their families. They also enjoy bringing in other personal "artifacts" such as copies of their birth certificates, library cards, favorite toys, or books. These objects can be placed in a decorated shoebox and when an individual student shares his or her box of artifacts, the other children learn about the student's life and interests, too.

As students get older, they can participate in an activity called "What's In Your Pocket?" This activity was adapted from a lesson from the website, Primary Source Learning. Students work in pairs with someone with whom they do not usually interact. The first student describes something in his or her pocket, purse, or book bag. The second student asks questions about it. Then, the second student hypothesizes about what the item tells about the first student. The second student justifies his hypothesis and students discuss if the hypothesis is correct. Students then switch roles so that each has an opportunity to hypothesize what can be learned from an object.

To extend the lesson, students who are studying the Civil War can examine the objects that were in Abraham Lincoln's pocket on April 14, 1865. Items in his pocket (and background information) are displayed at the Library of Congress America's Story site. To view this on the Internet, perform a search using the words, "Library of Congress and Lincoln's pockets." While ordinary objects such as glasses and a wallet were in his pocket, students enjoy surmising why he also carried a $5 Confederate note. The use of the pocket can be extended to objects that might be in the pockets of other historical figures. It can also be used with characters in historical fiction. After reading *Johnny Tremain* by Esther Forbes, students think about what would be in the pocket of the apprentice (Johnny Tremain), the merchant (John Hancock), a master craftsman (Paul Revere), or any of the female characters such as Priscilla Lapham, Miss Lavinia, or Mrs. Bessie. Then, students can recreate their character's pocket and justify each item they include.

Another extension of the "What's in Your Pocket?" activity is gathering and creating objects for a fanny pack. This engaging activity is from Professor Dennis Dennenberg, retired from Millersville University. At the conclusion of a biography unit, or a unit on heroes, and after students have thoroughly researched the accomplishments of a notable individual, they each create a fanny pack of object replicas, and pictures or documents that provide significant information about a person's life. Rather than writing reports, students assemble items to be placed in fanny packs. Individual students present their packs to their classmates and reveal one item at a time, being prepared to justify the inclusion of each object. Classmates in the audience try to guess the individual. A sample pack for George Washington Carver might include the following:

- peanuts (Carver discovered over 300 uses for the peanut.)
- cotton (Cotton crops depleted the soil, so Carver sought ways to diversify crops.)
- soybeans (Carver invented a process for producing paints and stains from soybeans.)
- test tube (This was one Carver's "tools" in the laboratory.)
- a quote: "Education is the key to unlock the golden door of freedom."
- a white flower (Carver always had one in his lapel pocket.)

- picture of a piano (He loved playing the piano.)
- picture of Carver with the faculty at Tuskegee University

Field Trips

Field trips enable students to expand their learning beyond the classroom. They provide students with experiences that cannot be recreated in the classroom but are nevertheless aligned with instructional objectives. Through these realistic experiences, students acquire information through active hands-on experiences and deepen their understanding of a topic. To prepare for trips, teachers discuss with students the purpose of the trip and provide the much needed background knowledge. This includes introducing vocabulary, displaying and discussing pictures, or providing time to explore the site's website. Students should also begin developing questions about the site as well as discussing examples of good questions for tour guides, docents, or reenactors at the site.

Depending on the purpose and type of trip, students might bring notebooks or sketchpads to record information. A teacher might also provide a scavenger hunt activity if the site does not have guides. During the trip, students need time to observe, ask questions, and reflect. After the trip, it is essential that students reflect on their experiences. Teachers should

- provide time for students to make general observations and reactions;
- ask students to compare the hands-on experience with what they have already learned;
- have students evaluate the most important display or object that they observed;
- create a classroom display of pictures, literature, and items students collected;

- give students an authentic summary activity such as having them write thank-you letters describing what they liked best about the trip and what they learned, or having them write an article for the school newspaper.

Internet Resources

Often, financial resources are limited and teachers cannot take students on field trips. There are also many places that are impossible to visit. In these situations, teachers can rely on virtual or electronic field trips. These trips are interactive and can be repeated often. An added benefit is that students can move through them at their own paces. One example of this is a virtual visit to the Tenement Museum in New York City. Students listen to an audio tour with the reading of primary sources as they "walk through" each family's apartment in the tenement. Many history sites now include virtual tours on their websites.

The National Park Service also has a website entitled Teaching With Historic Places. Materials provided at this website enable students to learn from places without leaving their classrooms. In over 130 lesson plans, students may examine and question readings, documents, maps, and photographs. Each lesson begins with an inquiry question and the activities enable students to connect these historic sites to the broad themes of American history. For instance, the materials in the lesson plan on Thomas Edison's Laboratories in West Orange, New Jersey, include readings and images. All of the activities lead students to consider the process of invention and its impact on society.

Classroom Museums

Students can also create their own museum exhibits. This authentic activity is often used as a culminating project. Prior to beginning the project, it is useful to visit a museum and discuss the work of curators and people who are responsible for displaying artifacts. Students should consider how objects are shown, examine the labels on the objects, note the descriptive information on the walls, and, if possible, talk with a curator or exhibit designer.

Then, working individually or in small groups, students will create objects as part of the culture or time period under study and design museum displays. If a class is concluding the study of ancient China, each child will select a topic and then an object from the society that interests them. They will then research the objects using some of the questions previously discussed and examine the use or impact of each one on Chinese society. Creating a model of the actual object can be done in class or as a homework assignment. Using actual museum labels as examples, students will write short labels for their objects including:

- object's name
- its composition
- its owner
- its use and importance in the society

The teacher might also want to assign an additional piece of written text for the object to be included in the museum's catalogue. Students work within the parameters assigned to create the artifact's display. When the museum is completed, parents and other visitors will be invited to see the displays. Students act as curators and explain their parts of the exhibition. They use additional information from their research to describe their artifacts.

This activity is an excellent interdisciplinary project. Students begin by picking topics in which they are interested. They use critical and creative thinking to research and design their objects. The labels and written text for the catalogue require them to utilize their writing skills, and finally, they hone their communication skills when families and friends tour the museum and ask them questions. In the process, they begin thinking like historians and museum curators.

The Smithsonian's Center for Education and Museum Studies and the Museum in Progress websites provide a more in depth explanation of how to create classroom museums.

Hands-on Geography

Before students in a world-geography course begin the study of a region, they should be exposed to a variety of geographic information to give themselves background knowledge for further in-depth study. This activity could easily be placed in the chapter on building background knowledge, but because of the variety of hands-on materials, it fits best in this chapter.

For a unit on the region of West Africa, begin with a classroom discussion. Ask students if they know the definition of a region. Record what students know. In most cases, students will not come with much background knowledge, and some may have misconceptions. To introduce the specific region, gather a wide variety of geographic information and give students ample time to examine it. Students need to have experiences with the tools of a geographer, so include a variety of maps such as physical and political, rainfall and vegetation, topographic, population-density, and transportation-and-trade-network maps. Students will also look at geographic databases containing land-use information or crop production levels, satellite images, and aerial photographs. While all this geographic information will be examined later in the unit in greater detail, an initial examination will generate interest in the students. When students have had time to examine the resources, developing a KWHL chart would be an excellent way of compiling information and generating questions to drive instruction. Students will discuss what they know about West Africa from the information they've examined, and generate questions for investigation (what they want to learn.) They will also discuss how they will gather the information, and from what sources. This is a crucial step in the process so students can think about ways to gain information. As the unit progresses, students will complete the last section of the chart, listing what they have learned.

For an added twist to this activity, trim the maps in such a way that students cannot identify the specific region or part of the world. In this example, do not tell students the name of the region. Let them use clues from the maps to guess what part of the world they are studying. At the end of the lesson, reveal the region to the students and review their ideas, modeling deductive reasoning skills.

Simulations to Learn Concepts

Simulations are designed with a particular outcome and are very engaging for students. They must support both the concept and the objectives that the teacher has developed.

Primary students must learn economic concepts such as wants, needs, barter, trade, producers, and consumers. They also learn about supply and demand, scarcity, opportunity costs, interdependence, specialization, resources (including natural, capital, and human), and goods and services. Amazingly, these concepts are not so challenging because students have personal experiences that enable them to make connections with their own lives. It is also important to ensure that students are able to use and apply the terminology they are learning in a number of situations.

A market-day simulation will enable students to apply their understanding. There are many primary books published on the topic of markets. An excellent one to begin the lesson would be *Saturday Market* by Patricia Grossman and Enrique O. Sanchez. Read it aloud and discuss examples of the concepts that have been taught. Then, explain that students will be involved in their own market-day simulation. Each student will be a producer of a good or service, as well as a consumer. Have students bring in something that they have produced, such as foods, small crafts, or drawings for the market-day simulation. On the day of the market, have students set up a "booth" on their desks and be prepared to sell and buy goods and services. Allow students ample time to participate in the simulation. At the conclusion, make sure the students debrief and discuss their experiences. Teachers can chart their experiences, ensuring that students can use the economic terms correctly in their discussions. Students may also draw pictures or write journal entries or small books about their experiences and relate them to their own lives.

Simulations to Learn About Events

Students also enjoy simulations of events in history. If the teacher wants students to understand the conditions and challenges of a trip to Jamestown, the students can become individuals on the *Susan Constant* under the leadership of the captain, Christopher Newport. Begin by blocking off a section of the classroom floor for the boat. The boat was actually a little bigger than a school bus. Discuss with students the reasons men went to Jamestown in 1607. Assign students roles such as Reverend Robert Hunt, John Smith, carpenters, crew members, one of the boys, and the gentlemen. Give students paper bags and tell them they can each bring one thing for the journey. Have them describe the item or draw a picture to put in the sack. When the teacher is ready to begin the simulation, they will have students board the ship via "a gang plank" and sit on the floor of the boat. Explain that they are sitting in the hold of the ship. Only the crew and boys can come onto the deck. The teacher should pretend that he or she is Christopher Newport and retell the experience. Include factual details such as the departure day (December 20, 1606), that there was no wind so the ships were stuck in the English Channel for six weeks and that they did not actually get underway until February. Have students sway back and forth to simulate movement of boat. Discuss hunger, mice and rats on the ship, crowded conditions, boredom, sickness, and storms. Provide a sample of hardtack. Explain how people on the ship (other than crew members) passed the days. Allow students a brief stretch when the ships stopped to pick up supplies in the Canary Islands and the West Indies. During the worst storm of all after leaving the West Indies, use a water bottle and spray students. When students arrive at the Chesapeake Bay, have students wait to leave ship (another two weeks) until a good harbor site is found. Before leaving the boat, also discuss where people will sleep and what they will eat. Open the bags and see if students can use anything they brought with them. Debriefing the activity is essential. Students should discuss their feelings during the voyage and when land is finally sighted, why there were no women, different roles of individuals, and space issues. Students should also individually process the information by writing journal entries or sending letters back to their families in England. Background information for this simulation can be found at the Jamestown/Yorktown website.

One activity that students can participate in is a game called Feudal Candy. The objective of the activity is to help students identify the order of societal rank and loyalties within feudal Europe. Students take on the roles of the king, nobles, vassals, and peasants. Teachers can use small candy pieces which will represent the harvest. This candy is distributed to the peasants. The vassals confiscate six candies from each peasant. From each peasant's payment, the vassal keeps one candy and gives five to his noble. The noble, in turn, takes two pieces of each vassal's payment and gives the remaining three to the king. When the activity is concluded, the students discuss their feelings, the problems faced by the peasants, the power of the king and nobles, and the feudal system's power structure. (Other items like pencils and stickers can be substituted for candy.)

This activity can also be adapted for American history students who must learn the impact of taxation and economics in causing the Revolutionary War. In this case, role identification cards are given in the following way: one card has *King George III* on it, two are labeled *members of Parliament*, two are labeled *tax collector*, and the rest are labeled *colonist*. The candy (or other chosen items) is distributed to the colonists. When it is time to send taxes to the Parliament, the tax collectors take the candy from each student until all the candy is collected. The king gets 50 percent of all the candy collected, the members of Parliament get three-fourths of what is left and the tax collectors divide the one-fourth that is left. Students usually get very upset that taxes were collected without their consent and discuss the problem of "No Taxation without Representation."

These activities were adapted from a lesson created by two teachers from Bath County, Virginia, and can be found in the Virginia Scope and Sequence document.

Simulations to Prepare for Life

Even for middle school and high school students, the study of economics needs to transfer from the abstract concepts to real life so that students can understand it better. Students understand economics when the concepts are directly related to what they know. To do this, assign a multi-week personal finance project. In this simulation project, students apply their knowledge of the roles of individuals in society, consumers and owners of resources, to a budget simulation. The objective of the simulation is to have students more fully grasp the choices people make in creating a budget given limited resources, opportunity costs, and cost benefits. Students purchase goods and services and keep track of their income and expenditures.

Organizing this simulation can be complex. Here's a brief overview to help teachers get started. To begin, students will draw identity cards that give their occupations and salaries. They will also assume that they are 25-year-old single individuals and that they are responsible for creating monthly budgets. Their budgetary choices will be dependent on their basic salaries and incomes. If the teacher wants to make the project more real, students should also be given information such as the miles they will drive to work, any debts that they might have, and other responsibilities. Information and choices will be recorded in separate sections of notebooks. This project will require students to conduct significant amounts of research from a variety of sources. Students will use information from newspapers, utility companies, insurance rates, retail catalogues, and information from their parents to complete the project. For each of their purchases, they will need to have the necessary cost documentation to support their choices. Students will be given the following categories that they must consider when creating a budget.

Salary and taxes—In addition to their monthly salaries, students must know how much they will need to pay in federal and state income taxes.

Housing—Assume that students will either rent apartments or houses or that they will be paying mortgages on condos or houses. Since this is a monthly project, they do not have to consider down payments for mortgages or deposits on rentals. However, students do need to consider the cost of utilities. If they choose to rent, then utilities (gas, water, trash collection, electricity) may be included. If they own their condos or houses, they would be responsible for paying the utilities. They may also each decide to have a roommate and divide the costs.

Transportation—Most students will want to own cars, so they must consider the monthly payments. (They may assume that they have saved money in the past, and have enough money to pay the 10 percent down payments.) In addition to the cost of the cars, students must consider car maintenance and set aside monthly allotments. They also need to pay car insurance and the weekly costs of gas and oil. If students feel they can take public transportation to their work locations, they need to consider the cost per ride. For the purpose of the assignment, however, they cannot rely totally on public transportation, but must have cars.

Food—In order to figure out food budgets, students must first plan their weekly menus. They can assume that they already have staples, such as sugar, flour, and spices. Once they have created their menus, they will use grocery ads and trips to supermarkets to get prices for their food. Students will also need to consider eating out at restaurants and include that information in their food costs. Finally, students must buy between five and seven household items, such as soap, toothpaste, and shampoo.

Clothing—Since most people do not buy clothes every week, for this project, assume that students will need to buy four outfits for work during the month. If they work in professions that require uniforms, they can assume that those will be provided, but they still need clothing for other occasions.

Furniture and household items—Assume that students already have some furniture. But to make the project realistic, students should buy one or two furniture items during the month. They must also realize that often they can buy furniture on credit and will have 24 months to pay for the items. The price of the furniture can be divided by 24 to obtain the monthly cost. If students want to buy televisions or electronics, they should know the total cost and again calculate the monthly installments.

Investments and savings—Students should budget small amounts for investments. They should buy savings bonds, invest in stocks, or simply put money in savings accounts.

Miscellaneous—Finally, students need to consider additional monthly expenses. Each will need a phone, cable, and Internet service. They will also need to allot small amounts (perhaps $30) for medical expenses and decide on entertainment budgets for activities such as movies, sporting events, and hobbies. They should set aside small amounts (between $20 and $40) for unexpected expenses such as dry cleaning bills, gifts, or repairs.

As students work through each part of this simulation, daily discussions are held so that students can debrief and share information. Teachers and students discuss the challenges they face relating to income levels. They use terminology that was outlined in the introduction to this simulation. Students can create journal entries as they progress through the different categories and reflect on their challenges and choices. Through these ongoing reflections, both the students and teacher can assess understanding.

This simulation was adapted from a project created by Anita Dienstfrey, Fairfax County Public Schools, Virginia.

Conclusion

History and the social studies are certainly more than dates, facts, and abstract concepts. Hands-on experiences for students help them bring meaning and engagement to what otherwise could be dull and mundane. Participation in authentic, active, and purposeful activities helps with the retention and understanding of the difficult concepts and ideas inherent in the disciplines. Teachers can use these ideas as a springboard to help them think of other possibilities for making social studies come alive for their students.

Chapter 7 Reflection

1. How do you make history and the social studies come alive for students?

   _____

   _____

   _____

   _____

2. Consider a unit in which you rely primarily on using text material. What hands-on strategies or activities might you add to your unit?

   _____

   _____

   _____

   _____

3. What challenges do you foresee? How can you address them?

   _____

   _____

   _____

   _____

   _____

   _____

Integrating Social Studies with the Arts

Recommendations on best practices in social studies advise teachers to decrease the time spent on textbook reading and test taking and increase the "integration of social studies with other areas of the curriculum" (Zemelman, Daniels, & Hyde, 1998, p. 155). The social studies come alive for students when teachers integrate them with other disciplines, especially the arts. Because the arts are a defining part of history that makes civilizations unique (Levstik & Barton, 2001), it is essential to integrate the arts into the classroom curriculums whenever possible. Teachers need to pick powerful literature, have students dramatize events, and imbed the art and music of a culture so that students will see the entire picture of what they are studying.

Many of the activities and strategies outlined in this book have shown how the social studies can be integrated with other disciplines. A large part of this volume has been devoted to the integration of history, geography, economics, and civics with reading, writing, speaking, and listening. In this chapter, a few specific strategies will be discussed that will help teachers further engage their students. ·

Connecting with Drama

In the social studies, students need to learn an enormous amount of information in a given unit of study. According to work summarized by Marzano, Pickering, and Pollock (2001), students need multiple exposures to details to learn them. Teachers provide verbal instruction and visual instruction, but the effects of dramatizations on learning are the greatest. With dramatizations, students can either observe a dramatization or participate in one. Using drama is highly motivating, and students learn to work cooperatively, do research, and apply critical thinking and problem-solving skills. It also is an opportunity for the teacher to tap into students' multiple intelligences and learning styles.

All students, from youngest to oldest, need to get up and move to get more blood pumping to their brains. This increases their attention spans and helps them think clearly. One way to do this is to have students act out concepts. At the primary level, students must understand a variety of geographic terms such as *hill*, *mountain*, *river*, *island*, and *peninsula*. After showing children pictures of these features, students create movements and rhymes to help them remember the feature's characteristics. Fourth graders studying their state's geography also need to know the characteristics of the regions. For example, Texas has four regions. An excellent way of internalizing the features of each region is to divide the class into four groups and have students dramatize what each region looks like and perform their dramatizations for their classmates. By observing and participating in these dramatizations, students internalize the features of the geographic regions.

To help students apply and synthesize information they have learned, teachers can have them role-play. For this activity, students take on the roles of others and view content from a variety of perspectives. They develop empathy for the people from a different period in time or location around the world. For example, to gain a greater understanding for the jobs of craftsmen during the colonial period, half of the students are given the roles of colonial craftsmen and the other half are customers in the shops. All students give themselves appropriate colonial names. Sample occupations include the cooper, wig maker, barber, printer, printer's apprentice, wheelwright, blacksmith, and cabinetmaker. Customers include the wives of plantation owners, members of the middle class, members of the gentry, free blacks, slaves, and other craftsmen. The teacher provides a wide variety of resources, so students are able to research their roles. Craftsmen learn about the products and services they provide and the kinds of tools and materials used. They give their shops names and understand why their shops were important in colonial America. Customers research their needs as well as means of payment for goods and services. Students may also create costumes and props and must plan for their role-play situations. When all is ready, students dramatize encounters in the shops. The teacher can also step back in time and interview the students in the shops. In this way, all the necessary information will be included.

At the conclusion of the activity, it is important to discuss and assess the role-play situations. Students discuss what they learned, how they felt about their roles and the roles of others, and the purpose of doing the activity and its value for increasing understanding of the colonial time period.

Another strategy that also makes a great culminating activity is called Living Statues. Students assume the roles of famous people in their state's history and each student creates a living statue showing what the person did in his or her life. Using masking tape, mark off the shape of the state in the classroom. Make a big enough map so a small group of students can stand inside of it. Have each student choose a person in the state's history and give each student time to review the accomplishments of the person and other important facts. Have a few students at a time stand in the map area and when the teacher says "freeze," they should assume a pose characteristic of the person. Then, the teacher should interview the students. Use an object to represent a microphone and a small reporter's pad. Tap the student on the shoulder to begin the interview. He or she will come alive and be the person. Have the student introduce the individual and explain why his or her person was important in the state's history. Ask additional questions that ensure that the critical information is presented. Students in the audience can also ask questions of the living statue.

Older students can even become the character. Often, when studying historical individuals, students focus on all aspects of the individuals' lives including family, events, and major accomplishments. For this reenactment, each student focuses his or her research on a specific moment in the individual's life. Alternatively, the focus may be on a decision made by that person, the reasons behind the decision, and its lasting impact. Students should also look for specific words spoken or written by their individuals. When they share their information with classmates, they become the individuals in much the same way as reenactors in Colonial Williamsburg or at other living history museums. They should remain in character while they are "onstage."

Connecting with Art

Art can be utilized in the classroom in two different ways. One way is to study art as a source of information. When examining Kente cloth from Ghana, pottery from the Hopi Indians, bronze vessels from China, and stone sculptures from Mexico, students learn about what is important to a people. They learn about their clothing, food, shelter, architecture, recreation, and technology. They also learn about their religious beliefs and values. Famous works of art often trigger emotions that words cannot. Think about the emotions portrayed by paintings of American Indians by George Catlin or the monumental landscapes of the romantic era painter, Albert Bierstadt. Analyzing art helps students make comparisons with their own lives and also leads to students asking more questions.

Consider the painting, *The Jolly Flatboatmen* by George Caleb Bingham. In this picture (Image 8.1), the characters are carefree, dancing, and playing music on the river. Bingham wanted to paint an energetic, optimistic picture of life in the west. However, students also need to address the question of whether or not this picture is realistic. The painting makes flatboat trips look easy. The men seem relaxed. What was the experience of transporting cargo on rivers really like? What were the challenges? Students need to make comparisons with what they read in textbooks and primary sources to answer these questions. They can also compare the exuberance in the painting with Walt Whitman's "I Hear America Singing" from *Leaves of Grass*. Finally, students can make comparisons to contemporary life and discuss how cargo is transported today.

Image 8.1: *The Jolly Flatboatmen* **by George Caleb Bingham**

Source: The Granger Collection, New York

The other way of using art is to produce it. This involves students in problem solving and creating and addresses their different learning styles. It is important for teachers to choose art activities with lesson objectives clearly in mind. Producing art is fun, but what is its purpose? Sometimes teachers want students to try their hand at weaving so they will understand how an artist created Kente cloth or to create and decorate a pot as a craftsman in ancient Greece might have done. Teachers might also ask them to artistically represent a concept that they have learned about. For instance, having students create drawings to represent their knowledge of the five freedoms in the First Amendment enables students to synthesize their understanding in an artistic format.

They must consider the five freedoms and why they are important and then find ways to symbolically depict their ideas.

Examining the architecture of a group of people also provides valuable information. Students gain geographic understandings by examining the kinds of materials used in creating the buildings, weather conditions, population density, and mobility issues. They study the shelters of people as well as the public structures they create. They also learn about peoples' values and religious beliefs, and study the impact of one civilization or group of people on another. To begin the study of buildings, the following questions could be asked.

- What is the location and setting of the building?

- For what purpose was it built?

- What are the building materials?

- What kinds of decorations and designs are on the building?

- What words or signs are on the building?

- What is the current use of the building?

- How does design reflect the values of the society?

If a group of students is studying the architecture and structures produced by the ancient Greeks or Romans, its study would include the Parthenon on the Acropolis, the Forum, Roman Coliseum, and aqueducts. In addition to the questions above, students would research buildings that are currently built in the same styles and ask why those styles are still copied today. Students get quite excited when they see buildings in their local communities that integrate architectural features used in ancient Greece and Rome. Teachers can pose the question, "What do these buildings tell us about our current values and beliefs?"

The government also produces works of art and students can both study the examples for information and then synthesize their knowledge by creating their own examples. Commemorative stamps and political posters are examples of this type of art. Public memorials and monuments are also created to honor individuals and the achievements of Americans. Often elementary-age children research famous individuals as part of a biography unit. Students can then create their own commemorative stamps depicting the individuals they have studied. They can synthesize their learning by writing letters to the United States Postal Service explaining the significance of the individuals in history and explaining why they feel a stamp should be created in honor of the person they studied.

Students also enjoy creating their own sculptures and monuments. This activity is used very effectively at the end of the year after students have studied a large time period of history. A teacher can introduce the lesson by showing students examples of various monuments and memorials. Some monuments contain actual sculptures of people, such as Abraham Lincoln in the Lincoln Memorial or Eleanor and Franklin Roosevelt in the FDR Memorial, both in Washington, D.C. Other memorials contain depictions of real people in historical events. A good example of this type of monument is the Korean War Memorial in Washington, D.C. Finally, some memorials are more symbolic such as the Vietnam Veterans Memorial and World War II Memorial in Washington, D.C. and the Statue of Liberty in New York Harbor. Students discuss the subject that the memorial honors, when it was made, and the values of the creators and the society. They then pick what they believe to be the most significant events or individuals that they studied during the year and design their own commemorative sculptures or memorials. Students use higher-leveling thinking skills to evaluate the people and events they have studied and create products that depict the significance of their subjects. In his book, *A Passion for the Past*, James Percoco gives additional examples of how he uses commemorative works with his high school students, and these ideas can easily be adapted for younger students.

Connecting with Music

Nothing engages students more than music. Teachers can use the music of a particular time period to help students understand what it was like to live back then. For instance, students may be listening to drumming and singing by Sioux Indians or traditional Japanese music using instruments such as the *shakuhachi*, *koto*, or *shamisen*. Using music this way helps students get a flavor for the time period and appreciate the customs of the people. Students can also listen to music and analyze the lyrics to better understand people's feelings during specific periods of history.

The protest songs of the 1960s can be used in middle school or high school while studying the Vietnam War. In the unit, students need to recognize the division of beliefs among Americans about the war as well as how domestic events influenced the foreign policy of the country. For this activity, divide the students into groups and provide each group with the lyrics to a song. For example, use the lyrics to songs sung by Bob Dylan and Joan Baez.

Have each group of students read the lyrics and then answer the following questions:

1. List the people, places, and events mentioned in the song.

2. What problems are addressed in the song? What are the exact lyrics that identify the problem?

3. Are there any repeated phrases? What are they? Why are these words important and repeated?

4. What is the tone or feeling of the song? What lyrics in the song make you think this?

5. What symbolism was used in the song? List the symbolism and its meaning.

6. Summarize the message or theme of the song.

7. Do you think this song is effective? Is the message clear? Why or why not?

When the groups have completed their analyses, discuss themes and symbolism. Look for common threads. Play the songs and let each group discuss the meanings of their songs so that everyone can benefit from all the songs. Use the answers to the questions to assess student understanding.

These questions and ideas were adapted from Fairfax County Public Schools in Virginia.

Connecting with Literature

While students often lament that textbooks are uninspiring and difficult to read, textbooks do give them needed background knowledge and a base from which to continue learning. However, picture books, biographies, novels, myths, legends, and even some nonfiction have voice and passion and bring history to life. It is important that teachers provide a variety of reading materials at a variety of reading levels so that students can become engaged with history. Students can read historical narratives to understand the emotions, fears, joys, challenges, and successes of ordinary and extraordinary people. As they read, they identify with the characters, make connections to their own lives, use their imaginations, and activate their curiosity. Through stories, myths, legends, and biographies, students become immersed "in times and cultures of the recent and long-ago past" (National History Standards, 1996).

When selecting a variety of narratives on a certain topic to use with students, Levstik and Barton (2001) use the following criteria:

- Is the book good literature and good history?

- Is the story accurate and authentic in details?

- Does it give a flavor of the times with somewhat authentic language?

- Is the historical interpretation sound?

- Are a variety of perspectives included?

- Can students make connections with their own lives?

In addition, it is important to make sure that a variety of books on different reading levels are included. Many informational books also give students insight into the lives of people. *Immigrant Kids* and *Children of the Wild West* by Russell Freedman are two excellent examples. Levstik and Barton also suggest the following criteria for choosing nonfiction books:

- What are the qualifications of the author?

- Are the facts accurate and complete?

- Is the book up-to-date and relatively current?

- Does the author distinguish between fact and supposition?

- Does the author provide notes for additional information and sources?

- Is the book well organized? Can it be used for different purposes?

- Are the author's voice and style apparent? Does the author seem to care about the topic?

While there are a wide variety of activities that can be used with literature, it is important that students understand that a single event can be described differently in different sources. When students see how different authors treat the same topics, they develop a deeper understanding of and respect for point of view and perspective in human experience (Blanchowicz & Ogle, 2001). If students are studying the Battle at Gettysburg, use graphic organizers to compare how different authors treat this event. One source of information is the textbook. Another is a nonfiction trade book such as *Eyewitness Reports: The Inquirer's Live Coverage of the American Civil War* by Edward Colimore and *Long Road to Gettysburg* by Jim Murphy. A third source, *Thunder at Gettsyburg* by Patricia Lee Gauche, uses poetic form to tell the story of a young girl in Gettysburg. Figure 8.1 shows students how to record information and personal reflections from three different sources.

Figure 8.1: Comparing Perspectives

Textbook	Nonfiction Source	Historical Fiction Source
Facts:	Additional facts:	Impressions and feelings of the characters:
Questions I still have:	Questions I still have:	Questions I still have:

Conclusion

Integrating social studies with the arts can be easily accomplished and is integral to the social studies. When studying history or the culture of other groups of people, the integration of the arts enables students to see the whole picture of different times and places. Some of the arts are primary source documents, while works created after an event reflect the vantage points of people interpreting a different time or place. They take students far beyond a textbook version of history and the social sciences. They provide a vehicle for student expression on a given topic and also help students make relevant connections to their own lives.

Additional Resources

Kelnor, L. B. (1993). *The creative classroom: A guide for using creative drama in the classroom.* Portsmouth, NH: Heinemann.

Percoco, J. (1998). *A passion for the past: Creative teaching in U.S. history.* Portsmouth, NH: Heinemann.

Social Education Magazine by NCSS provides yearly "Best Books in Social Studies."

Chapter 8 Reflection

1. How could you integrate more drama into a specific unit of study?

    _____

    _____

    _____

    _____

2. Consider the literature for a specific unit. Identify two fiction books and two nonfiction books that present varying perspectives on the topic. How will you use them in your instruction?

    _____

    _____

    _____

    _____

3. What is another example of how you could integrate art and music into a unit that you will be teaching?

    _____

    _____

    _____

    _____

    _____

Using Technology in the Classroom

Not too many years ago, teaching technology meant 16 mm projectors, slide projectors, and tape recorders. Today's students and teachers have moved far beyond that realm to classrooms with computers, Internet access, CD and DVD players, and telephones. Technology, like any innovation, has its positive and negative aspects. At the onset of the standards movement in the mid-1990s, most school districts and states embraced technology standards that, in a large part, addressed the "how to" components of using new technologies—specifically computers. Students were taught word processing and database and spreadsheet development and use with relatively little application. As time passed, students moved beyond the nuts and bolts of using word processing or spreadsheets and were taught how to use technology for the production of products such as multi-media presentations. These presentations included downloaded music, video clips and images, and collections of data designed to support a point of view. They could also be used as a means to gather information in order to solve a problem.

Many teachers today began using technology to teach content in their classrooms by using interactive simulations, such as the Oregon Trail where students "experience" the migration virtually, making decisions faced by those who actually did make the trek about what to bring, how to allocate resources, etc., reaching the ultimate goal of successfully completing the journey. As schools were wired to allow speedier access to the Internet, online versions and WebQuests replaced these packaged simulations. The benefit of these simulations, in addition to being fun, is the ability to spark students' thinking and learning about a particular event or time period. Technology can be used as a learning tool that moves beyond the idea of simulation to examples of its use for student and classroom investigation, research, and learning. This chapter will focus on learning with technology, not about technology.

What Does the Research Say?

A 1996 report titled, *Getting America's Students Ready for the 21st Century*, from a committee appointed by President William Clinton concluded that there were indications that students who engaged in the use of technology as a means of constructing their own knowledge were more consistently using the top three levels of Bloom's taxonomy than many of their counterparts who either did not have access to computer technology or were not using computers as tools for learning. The researchers were quick to admit that the research was inconclusive due to the fact that funding for the type of research to provide better data was critically underfunded and, thus, was not being carried out in any significant aspect. That said, experience shows that teachers who do have easy access to technology and who are well trained in using computers and other technologies as tools for learning are much more likely to develop lessons and projects that challenge their students to use technology to aid them in their development of critical thinking skills. For this reason alone, it is imperative that all schools, especially those that are economically disadvantaged, have the same opportunities across the nation. To make this possible, more government funding and private donors are needed.

Film, Video, CD, and DVD

Videos, and more recently DVDs, are a technology long used in social studies classrooms at all levels throughout the United States. Living in a culture where students have constant exposure to film and television, it is only natural that the genre be used in the classroom. A great production can spark a student's imagination and desire to learn more about what was just seen. All too often, however, "film" gets used to entertain or as a chance for an overwhelmed teacher to get some extra grading or paperwork completed as students watch. Another common practice is to show an entire video, stopping it throughout to talk with students about what they are seeing and learning and its relationship to what is being studied. The latter example is a more effective use of video, but most teachers agree that a short clip or set of clips from a video is the most effective method of all. Figure 9.1 is a planning tool for showing video clips or segments based on the work of Dr. Ted Green of Webster University and adapted from the work of Wiggins and McTighe (1998). This teacher tool is intended for use prior to showing the film clip or video segment to students.

Figure 9.1: Guided Viewing Planning Template

Guided Viewing Planning Template

Part 1: (Repeat Part 1 for each section of the film or film clip being viewed.)
- What is (are) the essential question(s)?
- Students will understand that ...
- Students will know ...
- Students will be able to ...
- Other

Part 2: Desired Outcomes (The following parts apply to the film/film clips as a whole.)
- Standards and grade level expectations
- Understandings: Students will understand that ...
- Essential question(s)
- Key knowledge and skill objectives
- Students will know ...
- Students will be able to do ...

Part 3: Assessment Evidence
- Performance task (include task's role, goal, audience, situation, product or performance, and standards)
- Key criteria
- Other evidence

Part 4: Learning Plan
- Learning activities and materials (texts, readings, documents, artifacts, websites, etc.) that will be used to supplement and enrich the film

---

Images are a powerful way to engage English language learners and many special-needs students. It is critical, however, that the image be analyzed and discussed by both student and teacher. Remember, too, the use of film as a means to offer students another perspective of an event or person being studied.

The care that is taken in choosing historical fiction that is meaningful and accurate for students should also be taken in the case of film. If the choice is made to show a film that is less than accurate in its portrayal of an event, it is incumbent upon the teacher to help students understand where the film diverges from what they know about that topic. Students should be made aware of what the inaccuracies are and, more importantly, how they find that information. Many of the questions suggested by Levstik and Barton (2001) listed in Chapter 8 for determining the value of a particular piece of literature could also be used with some adaptation for selecting video and film.

Microsoft® PowerPoint®

PowerPoint presentations are another effective use of technology to present images and text to aid student learning. Teachers can assemble a series of images (primary sources, in particular) designed to introduce a lesson or to present competing points of view of a given event. Displaying this *PowerPoint* presentation in a timed, looping manner as students enter the classroom piques interest and can serve as a hook to engage them in an upcoming lesson or unit.

PowerPoint presentations that mirror a lecture offer several advantages for students as they learn to take notes while listening to the teacher. It is important to remember that for the purposes of learning, lectures should rarely if ever last more than about 10 to 15 minutes without a break designed for students to process the information they are being given. A visual presentation that accompanies a lecture and highlights the important points being discussed helps students hone their note-taking skills and can be used to pose questions to guide student processing of information. It is particularly effective if slides are incorporated into the presentation. The slides will motivate students to think about what they have just learned and turn to partners or tablemates and share their thinking (think-pair-share). It is also effective if a question or questions precede an image or video clip that has been inserted into the presentation. Finally, and this has application far beyond *PowerPoint* presentations, when asking students about questions they may have regarding what they have just heard or learned, asking them "What questions do you have?" presupposes that they will indeed have questions and serves to further the discussion. Asking if students have questions generally leads to a nonresponse or a simple "No," thus ending the discussion.

WebQuests

WebQuests have long been used by teachers to teach students how to use the Internet while at the same time learning content and practicing their critical thinking skills. The result of its longevity is a wide range of WebQuests prepared by teachers throughout the United States that address the complete spectrum of content. It is important that when choosing a ready-made WebQuest, teachers thoroughly review and evaluate the lesson, objectives, and sites to be visited by students prior to undertaking the activity. The other alternative is to prepare a WebQuest oneself. The format follows a specific process that is easily adapted to almost any content and grade level.

Ready-Made Lessons on the Web

Undoubtedly, one of the richest sources for lessons can be found on the Internet. Teachers can save themselves a significant amount of time in not reinventing the wheel by finding a lesson that can be adapted to suit their needs. However, just as there are fabulous lessons to be found, there are equally poor ones in abundance. In keeping with the overarching theme of this chapter, be a wise consumer of the offerings that technology affords us.

When selecting a lesson found on the Web, make sure it tightly aligns to the standard, learning goal, objective, content, and skills of what students need to learn. Most lessons found on the Web will not align exactly to every teacher's needs. However, lessons can be adapted to fit most instructional plans.

One site that contains exemplary lessons, among the strongest to be found online, is the Learning Page of the Library of Congress's American Memory collection (http://www.loc.gov). This site contains lessons written by teachers that address a wide variety of topics as well as grade levels. The strength of these lessons is that they are directly linked to the items found in the more than 120 digitized collections of the Library. Each one of the lessons uses primary-source documents as its foundation. The Learning Page also contains a variety of analysis tools that may be used to help students evaluate different primary sources.

Another powerful site is the National Archives and Records Administration's Digital Classroom (http://www.archives.gov). The site contains lessons written by teachers who have attended summer workshops that trained them to find and use primary sources from the Archives' collections. The Digital Classroom also links to and supports National History Day. Like American Memory, the Digital Classroom has a collection of analysis tools that can be used online or downloaded for students and teachers. Lessons on this site have also been written by teachers and used in their classrooms. Lee Ann Potter, who heads this project, regularly publishes primary sources and an accompanying lesson in the issues of *Social Education Magazine*, the journal of the National Council of the Social Studies.

Last, but certainly not least, is the Gilder Lehrman Institute for American History's collection of lessons. Again, teachers who have attended summer sessions and produced lessons that use sources from its collection write the lessons. In addition, teachers can sign up online to receive electronic copies of a monthly lesson that is differentiated by grade levels and is prefaced by an essay written by historians who are experts in that area of study. Gilder Lehrman also supports the Organization of American Historians' *Magazine of History* by publishing a lesson relating to the topic of that particular issue of the magazine containing primary sources from their collection. Visit http://www.oah.org for information.

How to Evaluate Websites

Evaluating websites is of critical importance when using the Internet for research and WebQuest purposes. A number of website evaluating tools as well as other resources are available on Kathy Schrock's website. This site contains evaluation forms for websites at all grade levels, virtual tours, weblogs, and podcasts. The forms ask viewers to evaluate the technical and visual aspects of the page and offer a summary of that evaluation, the content, the authority (who created the page, the organization that sponsors it, etc.), and produce a narrative of the evaluation. The evaluations can be downloaded and printed or used online. Figure 9.2 is a re-creation of Kathy Schrock's elementary level website evaluation.

Figure 9.2: Elementary Level Website Evaluation

Name _____

1. How are you hooked to the Internet?

    _____ Modem and phone line

    _____ Direct connection at school/home

2. What Web browser are you using?

    _____

3. What is the URL (address of the Web page you are using)?

    _____

4. What is the name of the site?

    _____

Figure 9.2 *(cont.)*

Part 1: How does it look?		
As you look at the questions below, put an X in the *Yes* or *No* column for each.	**YES**	**NO**
Does the page take a long time to load?		
Are there big pictures on the page?		
Is the spelling correct on the page?		
Are the author's name and e-mail address on the page?		
Is there a picture on the page that you can use to choose links?		
Is there information in columns on the page?		
If you go to another page, is there a way to get back to the first page?		
Is there a date that tells you when the page was made?		
If there are photographs, do they look real?		
If there are sounds, do they sound real?		
Part 2: What did you learn?		
As you look at the questions below, put an X in the *Yes* or *No* column for each.	**YES**	**NO**
Does the title of the page tell you what it is about?		
Is there an introduction on the page telling you what is included?		
Are the facts on the page what you were looking for?		
Would you have gotten more information from an encyclopedia?		
Would the information have been better in the encyclopedia?		
Does the author of the page say some things you disagree with?		

Figure 9.2 *(cont.)*

Does the page lead you to some other good information (links)?		
Does the page include information you know is wrong?		
Do the pictures and photographs on the page help you learn?		

Part 3: Summary

Looking at all of the questions and answers above, write a paragraph telling why this website is helpful (or not helpful) for your project.

Kathleen Schrock. *"Critical Evaluation of a Website—Elementary School Level." http://school.discoveryeducation.com/schrockguide/*

There are also a number of articles written by Schrock and others about using the Web in classrooms, teaching students to conduct research using the Web, and criteria for evaluating Web pages, to name a few. Keeping a notebook that contains both teacher and student evaluations is an easy way to track sites and a good reference. It is critical, however, that teachers check sites at least at the beginning of each school year, if not more often, to make sure the sites are still available and safe for students.

Another fine site that supports the use of computer technology for classroom learning (among many other things) is History Matters, supported by George Mason University in Northern Virginia. The "Reference Desk" at this site offers information on citing digital resources, copyright and fair use, and evaluating digital resources.

Another important recommendation for using websites is that teachers can hot link them to their own Web pages or (for those less tech-savvy) create a word document on their computers that contain links to the sites they wish students to use. This eliminates students mistyping in URLs and ending up somewhere you had not intended for them to be.

Students Using Computer Technology

The emphasis in this chapter is on technology as a tool. It goes without saying that students are probably far more able and adept at using the latest technology than most teachers. Nevertheless, it is important to carefully plan student projects that use technology. Teachers need to talk with their students about the importance of doing their own work and not just cutting and pasting. They need to be discriminating users and realize that the Web represents only one venue for research.

One of the most frequently reported frustrations with students conducting Internet research is that students often need one-on-one attention just to search. In a typical class of 30 students, 29 of them are "on hold" while the teacher assists the one who needs help. There are several solutions to this problem that are useful and also offer a learning opportunity. One way to combat this is to have the class think about the terms they might use to search. This should take place prior to going to the media center or wherever students might be doing research. Ask students, individually, to list the subject headings they might use to research their topics. Then, ask students to share their search terms with partners or a group of students and brainstorm other search terms that they might use. If necessary, students can share their ideas with the entire class, who can then brainstorm other search terms. Students are instructed to write down their terms for later use. Encourage students to make sure that each search term is correctly spelled. When students get to the media center to do their research, each will have a number of subject headings they might use in a Boolean search that they can try prior to asking for individual help from the teacher. The added bonus of such an exercise is that it promotes creativity and divergent thinking on the part of the student that transfers beyond the trip to the media center.

Most importantly, teachers must constantly monitor the computer screens. Many labs today are set up so that the teacher can view a room full of students working simultaneously on computers from a central point. If that is not the case in a building, teachers can roam around the room looking over students' shoulders. Students are curious and can inadvertently mistype the URL. Young students in the early grades to middle school need a specific list of sites they might visit. As students reach the middle grades, a bit more autonomy is recommended. For example, the teacher might be using the Library of Congress's American Memory site and instruct students that they can "go" anywhere the links from the Library take them. High school students should be expected to use the Web as one of many research tools, but they also need to have their boundaries clearly defined, articulated and understood. Many schools already have an Internet use "contract" or form for students and parents to sign acknowledging the policies of computer and Web use. If a school does not have such an instrument, teachers may want to devise one of their own.

Conclusion

To not use technology in the classroom in this day and age is doing a great disservice to students in preparing them for what lies ahead. While the abundance of technology available today is unprecedented, it is wise to remember that it should be used as a tool for teaching the content and skills students must master. It is important to be thoughtful and deliberate as teachers plan and implement lessons that use technology as a vehicle for learning to insure that it's being used effectively and with purpose.

Additional Resources

Carnes, M. C. (1996). *Past imperfect: History according to the movies.* New York: Henry Holt and Company.

Harris, J. (1998). *Design tools for the Internet-supported classroom.* Alexandria, VA: Association for Supervision and Curriculum Development.

Silver, H. F., Strong W., Perini, M., & Reilly, E. (2001). *The interactive lecture: Research-based strategies for teachers.* Woodbridge, NJ: The Thoughtful Education Press.

Chapter 9 Reflection

1. Consider your current use of technology. Identify the ways you will incorporate strategies found in this chapter.

   _____

   _____

   _____

   _____

2. What challenges do you face in using technology in your classroom? How will you meet and overcome them?

   _____

   _____

   _____

   _____

3. What ideas do you have for adding technology to the tools you use in your classroom? How will you go about implementing those ideas?

   _____

   _____

   _____

   _____

   _____

   _____

   _____

Assessment

In today's environment and culture of high-stakes testing, pressure to demonstrate success through test scores and other numbers has given the idea of assessment a somewhat negative connotation. Comments about "teaching to the test" spoken with derision abound. The unfortunate result in all of this is that the importance of assessment for student learning has been somewhat undermined by this need to provide proof of student learning. The irony is that if assessment for learning is used effectively as a means to inform instructors and students of their progress, then student success on the assessment of learning will naturally follow.

Typically, the assessment of learning is considered summative while assessment for learning is diagnostic or formative. It is important to keep in mind that a single assessment could measure both types of learning if structured for that purpose. Generally, however, the assessment will probably lean more in one direction than the other. See Figure 10.1.

Figure 10.1: Assessment OF and FOR Learning

Assessment OF Learning	Assessment FOR Learning
• Checks what has been learned to date	• Checks learning to decide what to do next
• Is designed for those not directly involved in daily learning and teaching	• Is designed to assist teachers and students
• Is presented in a formal report	• Is used in responding to student work and in conversation
• Usually summarizes information into marks, scores, or grades	• Usually detailed, specific, and descriptive feedback in words
• Usually compares the student's learning to either that of other students or the "standard" for a grade level	• Usually focused on improvement, compared with the student's previous best/progress toward a standard
• Does not need to involve the student	• Must involve the student—the person most able to improve the learning

Assessment Drives Instruction

No matter which type of assessment is being administered, its relation to planning instruction is the first consideration. An ongoing nature exists in the realm of assessment. Too often teachers teach the content or concepts and believe that their students have understood what was taught. Often the time constraints placed on teachers by outside sources pressure them to move along. However, students who have not mastered the material will not successfully move on. Thus the question becomes, how do teachers know their students have gotten it?

Assessment that drives instruction is cyclical in nature. Teachers identify the place where they begin by knowing where it is they want to end. Wiggins and McTighe (1998) refer to this process as backward planning.

- What are the steps necessary to master the content and skills being taught in the lesson?

- What are the means to know if students are learning it along the way instead of waiting until the end to find out they missed the point?

- What do I do if, along the way, I realize that students have not learned what they need in order to move to the next part of the lesson or level of understanding?

The answers to these questions come from an understanding of how teachers think about lesson planning and assessment. The questions in Figure 10.2 show how teachers think as they plan lessons or activities. When planning, do teachers think more like an assessor or an activity designer?

Figure 10.2: Assessor or Activity Designer?

Thinking Like an Assessor	Thinking Like an Activity Designer
• What would be sufficient and revealing evidence of learning and understanding? • What performance tasks must anchor the unit and focus the instructional work? • How will I be able to distinguish between those who really understand and those who do not (though they might seem like they do)? • Against what criteria will I distinguish the work? • What misunderstandings are likely? How will I check for them? What will I do if I find any?	• What would be interesting and engaging activities on this topic? • What resources and materials are available on this topic? • What will students be doing in and out of class? • What assignments will be given? • How will I give students a grade and justify it to their parents? • Did the activities work? Why or why not?

The strength of Wiggins and McTighe's planning-backward process is that it helps move teachers toward thinking as assessors when they are planning activities and lessons. The question as to how they will know that the student has mastered the material will be at the forefront rather than as a parenthetical ending. This kind of thinking affects the kinds of activities and assignments that are planned for a lesson. It also helps teachers hone in on what students need to learn and be able to do as well as how to be deliberate in the methods they use to accomplish that goal.

Models for Constructing Assessments

The information found in Figure 10.3 serves as a means for thinking about a lesson from the perspective of an assessor. Consider the following questions and how they would be answered using the information provided in Figure 10.3.

- What is the purpose of my lesson or activity? (Mastery of content? Reasoning? Skills? A combination?)

- How will I most effectively measure the learning of my students, the degree to which they have met my goals? (Selected response? Products? Performance assessment? Personal communication? A combination?) How will I communicate their progress to my students? To their parents?

- What learning activities will I develop to help students use the content to practice the skills or reasoning that I will be assessing?

Responses to these questions enable teachers to begin to think about the strategies and tools they will use to measure student progress. Remember, the type of assessment teachers use to gather data about student learning needs to be compatible with the purpose of the assessment. In other words, selected response items such as true and false or multiple choice will not yield much, if any, information about your students' abilities to develop an historical thesis based on a set of documents. Thus, if the purpose of a lesson is to teach students to analyze documents in order to answer an historical question prompted by the material they contain, a selected response would not inform the teacher as to the students' abilities to use that process.

Figure 10.3: Achievement Targets and Assessment Methods

	Mastery of content	Reasoning	Skills
Selected response (multiple choice, true-false, etc.)	Can be used to assess content knowledge— as can all five formats	Can be an excellent way to access some key kinds of reasoning—but not all kinds	Can only test for mastery of prerequisite procedural knowledge
Constructed response (short answer, time line, visual representation, etc.)	Can be used to assess student ability to reconstruct knowledge and apply it to a new situation	Can be used to assess some kinds of reasoning related to student ability to use knowledge	Can be used to analyze student use of knowledge to construct new understanding
Products (essay, portfolio, model, etc.)	Can serve to assess student mastery of complex structures of knowledge	Can provide a window into reasoning	Can ask students to describe the complex "how to" procedural knowledge
Performance assessment (oral presentation, simulation, debate, etc.)	Unless carefully constructed with a solid rubric, may not be as effective as the other three methods	Can watch student in the process of problem solving and draw inferences regarding proficiency	Can observe and evaluate skills as demonstrated

Figure 10.3 *(cont.)*

	Mastery of content	**Reasoning**	**Skills**
Personal communication (oral questioning, observations, interview, etc.)	Can assess small domains of knowledge when short-term record keeping is required	Can ask student to "think out loud" to examine problem solving proficiency	Can be a strong match when the skill is oral communication proficiency; can ask student to describe and discuss complex "how to" procedural knowledge

Figure 10.4 lists the various activities that can be used as the basis for an assessment. Note that the table separates the selected response items from the other four categories in terms of performance-based examples. Those items require a strong rubric that clearly delineates what is being assessed. Alignment of the assessment to the learning goal is critical. Teachers tend to confuse the learning aspects with production aspects. If teachers want their students to describe and defend the criteria that they have used to define a particular geographic region, the color of ink used, or the neatness or appearance of the product should not be a part of that assessment. Hence, the need for a rubric that clearly defines what the learning looks like.

Figure 10.4: Ways to Gather Data about Student Learning

Options for Formative and Summative Assessments				
Selected response items	Performance-Based Assessments			
	Constructed response	Products	Performances	Personal communication
Multiple choice True-false Matching Fill in the blank • words • phrases	**Short answer** • sentence(s) • paragraph(s) • label a diagram "Show your work." • time line **Visual representation** • web • concept map • flow chart • graph/chart • matrix • illustration • Venn diagram	paragraph/essay research paper log/journal poem story/play news article or editorial letters portfolio art exhibit model video/audiotape spreadsheet *PowerPoint* presentations	oral presentation simulation dramatic reading enactment debate demonstration skit/play songs	oral questioning observations interview conference process description "think aloud" learning log anecdotal notes

Adapted from Jay McTighe and Steven Ferrara, 1994.

Checklists and Rubrics

Before discussing the development of a rubric and what it entails, it is wise to consider exactly what a rubric is and how it differs from a performance-task assessment list that is commonly referred to as a rubric.

A performance-task assessment list provides an alternative to a rubric. It is a set of criteria that have assigned point values. These assessment tools resemble the checklists teachers used to attach to projects or papers after students turned in their work. Often, in addition to some measurement of learning, these assessment tools define the quality or components of appearance: color of ink, number of pages, use of grammatical conventions, etc. Often, however, the product components are given as much, if not more, value as the indicators of learning. Sharing such a checklist with students prior to an assessment is valuable to both the student and teacher. Questions to consider when creating a performance task assessment list include the following.

- What is the content knowledge needed to demonstrate mastery?

- What are the process skills students need to be successful?

- What are the components of the performance task?

- How many points will be allocated to each component?

To realize the performance-task assessment list's greatest potential, teachers need to provide students with models of student work that illustrate the full continuum (acceptable and not acceptable). An additional value of the performance-task assessment list is that it allows the teacher to differentiate instruction by changing the components listed on the task list or by adjusting the number of points assigned to a specific component.

A rubric is an objective set of criteria expressed as a scale and used to assess levels of student performance in comparison to clearly articulated standards. It is distinguishable from other forms of criteria in that a narrative describing the components that meet each level of performance accompanies each performance level on a rubric. Rubrics can be either holistic or analytic.

- Holistic rubrics give one rating for the work. They are fine for summative assessment where the student will not be given the opportunity to learn from the feedback.

- Analytic rubrics give individual ratings for components of the work. They are more useful to students in identifying areas for improvement.

Rubrics can be generic or task specific. The importance of models of student work, also known as anchor papers, that illustrate the differences in the levels used in the rubric cannot be overstated for the effective use of rubrics. The rubrics not only provide models for students to emulate, they also clarify distinctions among the levels of performance.

For the purposes of the following discussion, here is a four-point rubric with levels defined as unsatisfactory, partially proficient, proficient, and advanced. A fifth point can be used to indicate that the student did not take the assessment. When creating a rubric, use the following guide.

- Begin with a description of the criteria that applies to the proficient student. Once that level has been defined, describing the performance of other levels becomes less difficult.

- Avoid counting criteria when possible. Often when numbers are used to differentiate between performance levels, the quality of the response or example can tend to suffer. Consider the dilemma of five mediocre examples versus three excellent examples. Has the student achieved the advanced level because there are more?

- Use anchor papers or models of student work representing each level of performance to help students understand exactly what is expected.

- Conduct a scoring conference where students are given the rubric and the anchor papers and asked to score each one and assign it a proficiency level. This gets students looking critically at the rubric and understanding the differentiation between levels.

- Involve students in the creation of the rubric. Share the struggle to articulate criteria that clearly indicate levels of quality!

- Encourage students to assess their own performances using the rubric.

- Develop a reflection guideline that prompts their thinking about their achievements and how they might be improved.

Consider the examples of rubrics (Figures 10.5–10.7) on the following pages in light of the previous discussion.

Figure 10.5: Historical Advertisement Rubric

	No indication of work	Unsatisfactory	Partially proficient	Proficient	Advanced
	0	1	2	3	4
Content of advertisement demonstrates student's broad understanding of historical concepts.					
Advertisement shows real connection to historical context.					
Advertisement contains all necessary information or facts.					
Concept is original, persuasive, and appealing to the audience.					
Information is well presented: effective, concise, and error-free.					
Artwork is creative, colorful, and neat.					

Adapted from Fairfax County Public Schools in Virginia

The first two items in the list of criteria address student learning.

- broad understanding of historical concepts
- real connection to historical context

The third through sixth items in the list of criteria address the product students are to make.

- contains all necessary information or facts
- original, persuasive and appealing to the audience
- well-presented: effective, concise, and error-free
- creative, colorful, and neat

If a student completed all the tasks and produced an advertisement that was persuasive and appealing in an effective, concise, and error-free manner with colorful, creative, and neat artwork, but demonstrated little understanding of the historical concepts and context, he or she could score a *meets standard* on the project. What is not determined is what standard was being measured.

Compare the rubric in Figure 10.5 to Figure 10.6.

Figure 10.6: Rubric for Information Processing

4	Analyzes information in detail, accurately and insightfully determining whether it is credible and relevant to a specific task
3	Accurately determines whether information is credible and relevant to a specific task
2	Makes some significant errors in determining whether information is credible and relevant to a specific task
1	Makes little or no attempt to determine whether information is credible and relevant to a specific task, or totally misjudges the relevance and credibility of information
0	No indication of work

Source: Arter & McTighe, 2001, p. 177

Consider the example given in Chapter 5, From Document to Thesis, in which students are given a series of documents to analyze and practice a process that takes them from analysis to synthesis in the form of developing an historical thesis that directs inquiry. Using the rubric in Figure 10.6 allows a teacher to assess and communicate in a fairly concrete manner the abilities of students to process the information they have been given from the activity.

The rubric in Figure 10.6 identifies the standard being measured, assesses the value of information, and articulates the gradations of student performance necessary to evaluate learning.

Be assured that it is not necessary to write a rubric for each assignment a teacher gives. Just as the previous rubric was applied to a specific assignment, a generic rubric, such as the one in Figure 10.7, can be used for a variety of assignments as long as both the teachers and their students understand what each descriptor means. Again, anchor papers that clearly delineate the differences between levels are essential for successful use of a rubric like the one in Figure 10.7.

When it is necessary to inform students and parents of the mastery of skills, which rubrics would be easier to use? Which ones would more accurately measure what students have learned as opposed to what students have produced? It is important to determine what it is being measured—learning or student product—and design the rubric accordingly.

Figure 10.7: Generic Information Rubric

Rubric for Information		Rubric for Information for Younger Students	
4	The student has a complete and detailed understanding of the information important to the topic.	4	The student understands the important information completely. The student knows details about the information.
3	The student has a complete understanding of the information important to the topic.	3	The student understands the important information.
2	The student has an incomplete understanding of the topic or misconceptions about some of the information.	2	The student does not completely understand the important information, or the student's thinking shows some mistakes about the information.
1	The student's understanding of the topic is incomplete, or the student has so many misconceptions that he or she cannot be said to understand the topic.	1	The student does not understand the important information. The student's thinking shows considerable mistakes about the information.
0	There is not enough information to make a judgment.	0	The student does not try to do the task.

Source: Marzano, 2000

Ongoing Strategies FOR Learning

The previous discussion of assessments could lead one to think that all assessments require a major amount of planning and execution. That is relatively true for summative (*of* learning) assessments. However, there are a number of quick, easy, effective, and ongoing assessments, most often (but not always) used *for* learning.

Exit Cards

As students leave the classroom, teachers can ask them to take a minute to reflect on a question or have the students tell what they learned (as opposed to what they did) during class. Each student must then give the teacher the card in order to exit the classroom.

If the concept of manifest destiny was being studied and the teacher wanted to know if students understood that manifest destiny was more than a just a slogan, that at its core was the notion that it was America's destiny to expand its borders from sea to sea, students could be asked to draw pictures, sketches, diagrams, or graphic organizers that would illustrate this meaning.

At this point, a teacher can physically group the students by those who understood the significance of the content or the concept being taught that day and those that show little, if any, understanding. Then, what teachers have is some additional baseline data about those students who may need more instruction. That data can be used as information for the monitoring of student progress and for informing oneself of the next steps of instruction.

Marzano (2000) suggests that the information on the exit card could be presented in a way not used to learn the material. In other words, if students read a passage and discuss it, they then should represent what they learned graphically through sketches, diagrams, drawings, etc. This process involves using an additional part of the brain, thus ensuring that the information has been more thoroughly learned.

Venn Diagrams

One of the most effective uses of Venn diagrams is as a means to visually assess student understanding of a concept or idea. Three circles may be used; however, for less complexity, begin with two circles.

To assess students' understanding of the political positions of the North and South over the course of the 30 years leading up to the Civil War, a teacher could give each student (or groups of students) two different colored circles; one labeled *North* and the other *South*.

Then, the teacher would ask students to place their circles in Venn-diagram form to illustrate the similarity of political positions at the following times.

- 1820—Missouri Compromise
- 1850—Fugitive Slave Act and Compromise of 1850
- 1854—Kansas-Nebraska Act
- 1860—Election of Abraham Lincoln

As the teacher gives the students dates and events, he or she can circulate around the classroom and look at the responses. This also offers an excellent opportunity to question students about their positioning of the two circles.

Note: In 1820, the circles will be very nearly on top of one another. With each subsequent date, students should move the circles farther apart until 1860 when there is a relatively small overlap (the South has not yet seceded and still recognizes the validity of the Constitution).

Student-Involved Assessment

Student achievement improves when students are involved in the assessment process, are required to think about their own learning and articulate what they understand and what they still need to learn (Black & William, 1998; Sternberg, 1996). Student involvement in assessment does not mean that students control decisions regarding what will or will not be learned or tested or that they will assign their own grades. It does mean, however, that students learn to use assessment information to manage their own learning so they understand how they learn best, know exactly where they are in relation to a defined learning target, and plan and take the next steps in their learning. Student-involved classroom assessment works like a mirror that students hold up to watch themselves grow, to help them chart and feel in control of their own success. It lets students know and accept that no one is an expert the first time they try something; rather, there is a learning curve that starts low and progresses upward.

Students are involved when they do the following:

- use assessment information
- make learning decisions related to their own improvement
- develop an understanding of what quality work looks like
- self-assess
- communicate their status and progress toward established learning goals

Students can complete the following:

- score work
- develop criteria
- know and apply strategies for improvement
- reflect: deciding what's next
- keep records
- communicate regarding progress
- practice assessment development

There are a number of simple ways for students to assess their own learning that informs the teacher, allowing for adjustments in the next day's instruction.

3-2-1

- 3 things I want to remember
- 2 things that are still a bit unclear
- 1 question I have

Square, Triangle, Circle

- something I am "square" with (I understand fully)
- points I want to remember
- something still circling around in my mind

Likert Scales

- Give students a continuum of 1 to 5 or 5 to 10 and ask them to mark their understanding of a concept or content. This can be done just once, or at the beginning of the lesson or unit and then again at the end of the lesson or unit.
- Leave room for questions and comments.

1	2	3	4	5
No understanding	Some understanding	Moderate understanding	Good understanding	Complete understanding

Example: Rate your understanding of the economic concept of scarcity.

Conclusion

It is important that teachers understand the importance and flexibility of the assessment *of* and *for* learning, particularly the latter. Remember that assessment is circular and ongoing and is key to effective instruction. Teachers need to begin by assessing their students' knowledge in order to build on that knowledge (diagnostic). They continue to assess as the instruction progresses in order to know that students are ready for the next step (formative). And, they assess to measure their students' mastery of a concept through the content they have taught them (summative).

Additional Resources

Popham, W. J. (2001). *The truth about testing: An educator's call to action*. Alexandria, VA: Association for Supervision and Curriculum Development.

Stiggins, R. (1994). *Assessing reasoning in the classroom*. Portland, OR: Assessment Training Institute, Inc.

Chapter 10 Reflection

1. Think about assessment *for* and *of* learning and identify assessments you have given that are examples of each.

_____

_____

_____

_____

2. Consider the assessments you just identified. Which of the achievement targets are they designed to measure?

_____

_____

_____

_____

3. Assess a rubric you currently use with respect to the discussion of rubric development found in this chapter. What might you need to change?

_____

_____

_____

_____

_____

_____

Putting It All Together

This book will conclude by discussing examples of lessons that integrate different disciplines and apply some of the strategies and content outlined in this book. The following two examples illustrate the concept of "working smart," and through these different methods of integrating instruction, students will have the opportunity to apply skills and thinking processes in an active, thoughtful manner.

Harriet Tubman and the Underground Railroad

This mini-unit on Harriet Tubman and the Underground Railroad integrates reading skills with the examination of art, primary sources, and music. Given time restraints, a teacher will have limited time to devote to this important part of history, so the question becomes, "How can teachers integrate as much as possible and still cover the essential objectives?"

The teacher will set up different learning centers and students will rotate through them looking for information about the Underground Railroad. Questions to guide the exploration are as follows.

- What was the Underground Railroad?
- What people were involved?
- What was the route?
- Why was it important?

The following items will be placed at each center. Questions similar to those in Chapter 5 will help students analyze the primary sources.

Image 11.1: *The Underground Railroad* **by Charles T. Webber**

Source: The Library of Congress

Image 11.2: Harriet Tubman

Harriet Tubman (1823 – 1913) nurse, spy and scout

Source: The Library of Congress

Figure 11.1: 1847 Broadside

$200 Reward

RANAWAY from the subscriber, on the night of Thursday, the 20th of September.

Five Negro Slaves,

To-wit, one Negro man, his wife, and three children.

The man is a black negro, full height, very erect, his face a little thin. He is about forty years of age, and calls himself Washington Reed, and is known by the name of Washington. He is probably well dressed, possibly takes with him an ivory headed cane, and is of good address. Several of his teeth are gone.

A reward of $150 will be paid for their apprehension, so that I can get them, if taken within one hundred miles of St. Louis, and $200 if taken beyond that.

WM Russell

ST. Louis, Oct. 1, 1847

Source: "$200 Reward. Ran away, subscriber . . . Five Negro Slaves." Broadside. 1847. Rare Book and Special Collections Division, African American Odyssey, Library of Congress.

Image 11.3: Underground Railroad Map

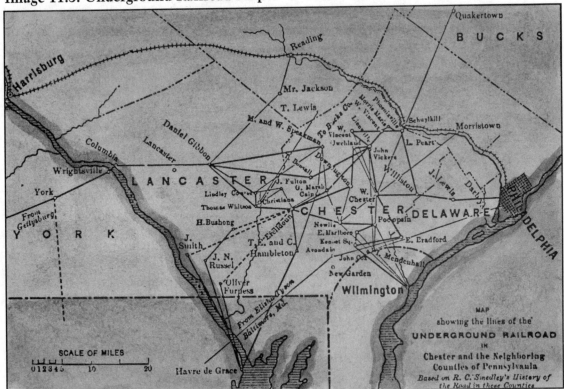

Source: The Granger Collection, New York

Other centers can include:

- Music and lyrics to the spiritual, "Go Down Moses" or "Follow the Drinking Gourd"

- Textbook passage on the Underground Railroad

- Picture books at varying reading levels to support different learning needs (Examples include *The Drinking Gourd* by Jeanette Winter or *Moses: When Harriet Tubman Led Her People to Freedom* by Carol Boston Weatherford.)

As students rotate through the centers, they will complete a data retrieval chart (Figure 11.2) listing information they learn from each source.

Figure 11.2: Data Retrieval Chart

Source	Paintings	Photograph	Poster	Music	Map	Textbook	Picture books
Facts							
Inferences							
Questions I have							

When students have completed their rotation through the centers, the concluding discussion will focus on the purpose of the Underground Railroad, key individuals involved, feelings of slaves and slave owners, and student reactions. Students will also discuss the points of view of the creator or writer of the different items at each center. They will compare and contrast information, share the inferences they made with each item, and evaluate the usefulness of each item in learning about the importance of the Underground Railroad. The teacher will informally assess participation in the discussions, completion of questions at each center, and information recorded on the data retrieval chart.

Using Water to Teach Civics, Economics, Geography, and History

The previous mini-unit demonstrated the integration of art, music, history, primary sources, literature, texts, and writing. The overview of the study that follows integrates the four social studies disciplines—civics, economics, geography, and history through the study of water. In this unit, the expectation is that teaching a global concept to students via the four disciplines will then enable students to apply those concepts to other contents.

The historical part of the study begins with a time line activity that asks students to think about the human development around a western river from the sixteenth century through the twenty-first century. Students, divided into groups, read brief histories of the land and the river at different points in time and are asked to portray that information graphically on a pre-prepared piece of chart paper that contains a portion of a river. When students combine their pieces of chart paper, they form a river time line that traces development over the course of five centuries.

The majority of the study focuses on economic concepts. Students experience a series of lessons and activities designed to teach them economic concepts that are key to understanding the issue of water. Included in those concepts are scarcity, opportunity costs and benefits, property rights, supply and demand, choice, incentives, Tragedy of the Commons, and the Diamond Water Paradox. Students learn these concepts in a variety of active, hands-on lessons by gathering data of their own water use, considering its uses and ways to ameliorate their thinking about how they value and use water. The role-play scenarios put them in the positions of various members of a community who use water for very different reasons. They take a step back in history to consider the importance of water to *Romeo and Juliet* as compared to diamonds and contemplate the reasons that diamonds are more valued than water. Students then explore the concept of property rights and how they apply to the use and ownership of water in various geographic areas of the United States. Finally, they look at the concept of diminishing marginal returns to determine at which point the cleaning of water is no longer economically advantageous.

After students have learned about the economic aspects of water, they undertake a study of water from a political perspective investigating related public policy and legal issues. They study the structure and function of government to better understand the groups involved in water issues and the various organizations, private and public, that are interested in water policy. Students then engage in a WebQuest to continue their study. Each student or group of students is given an identity that reflects one of the stakeholder's interest in water. Students research water issues from their stakeholders' perspectives and prepare presentations before a legislative hearing committee to present solutions to the water issue and defend their points of view. The WebQuest is also designed to allow students to practice the assessment for the unit in groups.

When the WebQuest presentations end, students are given the performance assessment that assigns them the role of president and CEO of a research company whose clients are interest groups throughout the state. Each student is to produce an action plan for his or her clients who wish to change public policy or solve a problem related to a particular issue. Students choose their own issues and apply the understanding of historical, geographic, economic, and political concepts they have learned. Specifically, students are asked to produce a time line that ties their issues to its nineteenth century antecedents and an overview that identifies a problem or issue existing in the state, discuss its background, and identify and describe the public policy in existence that relates to the issue. Students are asked to prepare proposals for making changes to the existing public policy or suggest several solutions to the problem. In that proposal, students are to discuss the economic concepts that apply to their solutions and identify and defend the solutions they believe best address the issues. Finally, students provide a list of agencies and organizations related to their issues, identify the levels (local, state, federal) of involvement, and explain how the interests of the agency or organization support their solutions.

A rubric that measures student understanding of each component of the assessment is applied to the project. The proficient student product is defined in Figure 11.3.

Figure 11.3: Proficient Student Attributes

Time line	• Time line illustrates all conventions (chronological order, spatial and scale considerations) • Time line events are relevant to issue • Includes events related to the issue from the nineteenth century to today
Overview	• Explanation identifies a particular problem or aspect of the issue as it exists in the state today • Relevant nineteenth century antecedents of the issue are identified • Public policy is related to the identified issue • Relationship between public policy and issue is accurately described
Proposal	• Proposal offers two or more alternative solutions to change the policy that are relevant to the chosen issues • Each solution identifies a relevant economic concept • Each solution discusses the relationship between identified economic concepts and the issue
Recommendation	• One solution is identified as "best" • Explanation contains the reasons why the choice was made • Recommendation indicates a plan of action to be taken that reflects the concept of citizen involvement in public affairs
Agencies	• A list of agencies and organizations related to the issues is included • Level (federal, state, local) of government or scope of organization is identified for most agencies or organizations • Explanation of each agency and how it relates to the issue is accurate in most cases

Conclusion

The expectations for exemplary instruction and student achievement are the norm in this culture of high-stakes testing. Teachers are expected to prepare their students for the specifics of state and national tests while at the same time engaging their students in the learning process. The social studies have traditionally been exciting, relevant, and hands-on. As time constraints for teaching the social studies have become tighter and tighter, it is incumbent upon teachers to find ways to teach the concepts and content in a manner that addresses and incorporates a variety of disciplines.

Additional Resources

Craver, K. (1999). *Using Internet primary sources to teach critical thinking skills in history*. Westport, CT: Greenwood Press.

Percoco, J. (1998). *A passion for the past: Creative teaching in U.S. history*. Portsmouth NH: Heinemann.

Vest, K. (2005). *Using primary sources in the classroom*. Huntington Beach, CA: Shell Education.

Chapter 11 Reflection

1. Consider a unit that you currently teach. What examples of music, art, literature, and primary sources could you use in this unit?

_____

_____

_____

_____

2. What lessons or units do you currently teach that can be adapted to include the content and skills of other disciplines?

_____

_____

_____

_____

_____

_____

_____

_____

_____

_____

_____

Glossary

assessment—process of gathering information about a student's achievement and ability

auditory learner—an individual who learns best by hearing information

authentic tasks—assignments or projects that are designed to assess students' abilities to apply standard driven knowledge and skills to real-world challenges

Bloom's taxonomy—a hierarchy of question types, ranging from knowledge-level to evaluation-level questions

case studies—a problem-based strategy that poses a problem from history for students to discuss and solve

concepts—mental constructs that are broad, abstract, universal in application, and represented by different examples that share common attributes

constructed response—a question or task in which students must create an answer or response themselves, but there is a set of information that is expected

constructivist learning—a learning environment where the students are the center and the teacher works as "the guide on the side"

cooperative learning—a teaching and learning approach in which students work together in pairs or small groups and learn from one another

diagnostic assessment—assessment used prior to instruction to determine a student's background knowledge

expository text—reading material that serves the purpose of providing information

formative assessment—ongoing assessment to make instructional decisions and determine progress toward goals

graphic organizer—a visual way to depict and categorize information

integration—the linking of content in different social sciences with different areas of curriculum

learning style—a method of learning that works best and is preferred by an individual

modeling—a teacher "thinks aloud" to introduce a skill or task

performance-based assessment—assessment that is based on observation and judgment of student-created products, demonstrations, or personal communication, which provide a portrait of student learning

primary source—original items or records that have survived from the past, such as clothing, letters, photographs, and manuscripts; part of a direct personal experience of a time or event

prior knowledge—information that the learner already has about a topic before the topic is introduced

problem-based learning—a curriculum development and instructional system that simultaneously develops both problem-solving strategies and disciplinary knowledge bases and skills by placing students in the active role of problem solvers confronted with an ill-structured problem that mirrors real-world problems

rubric—a guide for scoring student performance; rules for scoring include descriptions of key characteristics of various levels of performance

secondary source—items written shortly after or long after an event took place

selected responses—a question or task in which students must choose what they believe to be the best or correct answer from a list of provided possibilities

social studies—the study of the social sciences that includes the disciplines of history, economics, geography, government, and civics, as well as anthropology, archaeology, law, philosophy, psychology, religion, and sociology

summarizing—a strategy used to help the reader or learner distill the most important facts or ideas from a passage

summative assessment—an assessment used to document a student's achievement at the end of a unit or course or an evaluation of the end product of a student's learning activity

tactile/kinesthetic learner—an individual who learns best through movement and touching

visual learner—an individual who learns best by viewing information

References

Allen, J. (1999). *Words, words, words: Teaching vocabulary in grades 4–12.* Portland, ME: Stenhouse.

Allen, J., & Landaker, C. (2005). *Reading history: A practical guide to improving literacy.* New York, NY: Oxford University Press.

Arter, Judith & McTighe, Jay. (2001). Scoring rubrics in the classroom: Using performance criteria for assesing and improving student performance. Thousand Oaks, CA: Corwin Press, Inc.

Bain, R. (2007). Organization of American Historians, Teaching American History Grant Session March 19, 2007.

Blanchowicz, C., & Ogle, D. (2001). *Reading comprehension: Strategies for independent learners.* New York, NY: Guilford Press.

Black, P., & William, D. (1998). Assessment and classroom learning. *Assessment in Education: Principles, Policy and Practice, 5 (March),* 7–68.

Buehl, D. (2001). *Classroom strategies for interactive learning.* Newark Delaware: International Reading Association.

Capps, K., & Vocke, D. E. (1991). Developing higher-level thinking skills through American history writing assignments. *OAH Magazine of History* 6(2). Fall.

Duke, N., & Pearson, D. (2002). Effective practices for developing reading comprehension. In A. Farstrup & S. J. Samuels (Eds.), *What research has to say about reading instruction* (pp. 205–242). Newark, DE: International Reading Association.

Eastman, G. (1995). *A new look at the American west.* Boulder, CO: Social Science Education Consortium.

Frayer, D., Frederick, W., & Klausmeier, H. (1969). *A schema for testing the level of concept mastery* (Working Paper No. 16). Madison: Wisconsin Research and Development Center for Cognitive Learning.

Gunn, A., Richburg, R., & Smilkstein, R. (2007). *Igniting student potential: Teaching with the brain's natural learning process.* Thousand Oaks, CA: Corwin Press.

Harvey, S., & Goudvis, A. (2000). *Strategies that work: Teaching comprehension to enhance understanding.* York, ME: Stenhouse Publishers.

Haycock, K. (1998). Good teaching matters: How well-qualified teachers can close the gap. Thinking K-16, Vol. 3, Issue 2.

Jeffco Public Schools. (2001). *Best practices in vocabulary instruction.* Jefferson County Public Schools: Golden, Co.

Jones, R. Vocabulary word map. Website: http://www.readingquest.org

Keene, J. (2006). "Unpacking the historical thinking behind the United States and the First World War." Kansas City, MO. Gilder Lehrman Institute, June 7, 2006.

Kobrin, D. (1996). *Beyond the textbook.* Portsmouth, NH: Heinemann.

Levstik, L. S., & Barton, K. C. (2001). *Doing history: Investigating with children in elementary and middle schools.* Mahwah, NJ: Lawrence Erlbaum Associates, Publishers.

Macceca, S. (2007). *Reading Strategies for Social Studies.* Huntington Beach, CA: Shell Education.

Macon, J. M., Bewell, D., & Vogt, M. (1991). *Responses to Literature.* Newark, DE: IRA.

Marzano, R. J. (2004). *Building background knowledge for academic achievement.* Alexandria, VA: Association for Supervision and Curriculum Development.

Marzano, R. J. (2000). *Transforming classroom grading.* Alexandria, VA: Association for Supervision and Curriculum Development.

Marzano, R. J., Pickering, D. J., & Pollock, J. E. (2001). *Classroom instruction that works: Research based strategies for increasing student achievement.* Alexandria, VA: Association for Supervision and Curriculum Development.

McTighe, J., & Ferrara, S. (1994). *Assessing learning in the classroom.* Washington, D.C.: National Education Association.

Moore, D., Moore, S., Cunningham, P., & Cunningham, J. (2006). *Developing readers and writers in the content areas K-12.* Boston: Allyn & Bacon.

National Center for History in the Schools. (1996). *National history standards.* Los Angeles: UCLA.

Ogle, D., Klemp, R., & McBride, B. (2007). *Building literacy in social studies: Strategies for improving comprehension and critical thinking.* Alexandria, VA: Association for Supervision and Curriculum Development.

Sternberg, R. (1996). *Teaching for thinking: Psychology in the classroom.* Washington, D.C.: American Psychological Association.

Sundem, G., & Pikiewicz, K. (2005). *American history activities.* Huntington Beach, CA: Shell Education.

Taba, H. (1967). *Teachers' handbook for elementary social studies.* Palo Alto, CA: Addison Wesley.

Taylor, R. (1994). *Strengthening English and social studies instruction: Using outstanding integrated, thematic teaching strategies.* Bellevue, WA: Bureau of Education and Research.

U.S. Department of Education. A Report to the Nation on Technology and Education. *Getting America's students ready for the 21st century: Meeting the technology literacy challenge.* June 29, 1996.

Vacca , R., & Vacca, J. (1999). *Content area reading: Literacy and learning across the curriculum.* New York, NY: Addison-Wesley Educational Publishers, Inc.

Vest, K. (2005). *Using primary sources in the classroom: Examining our past, understanding our present, considering our future.* Huntington Beach, CA: Shell Education.

Wakefield, L. (2003). "Creating reader's theater: A poem for two voices." Fairfax, VA. NCHE Colloquium, February 19, 2003.

Wiggins, G., & McTighe, J. (1998). *Understanding by design.* Alexandria, VA: Association for Supervision and Curriculum Development.

Wyman, R. (2005). *America's history through young voices: Using primary sources in the K–12 social studies classroom,* Boston. MA: Pearson Education, Inc.

Zemelman, S., Daniels, H., & Hyde, A. (1998). *Best practice: New standards for teaching and learning in America's schools.* Portsmouth, NH: Heinemann.

Zola, J. (1996). *Sand creek: Battle or massacre? A new look at the American West.* Boulder, CO: Social Science Education Consortium.

Additional Resources

Beers, K. (2003). *When kids can't read—What teachers can do.* Portsmouth, NH: Heinemann.

Benjamin, A. (1999). *Writing in the content areas.* New York, NY: Eye On Education.

Billmeyer, R., & Barton, M. (1998). *Teaching reading in the content areas: If not me, then who?* Alexandria, VA: Association for Supervision and Curriculum Development.

Blanchowicz, C. (2005). *Teaching vocabulary in all classrooms.* Upper Saddle River, NJ: Prentice Hall.

Carnes, M. C. (1996). *Past imperfect: History according to the movies.* New York: Henry Holt and Company.

Clark, S. (2007). *Writing strategies for social studies.* Huntington Beach, CA: Shell Education.

Craver, K. (1999). *Using Internet primary sources to teach critical thinking skills in history.* Westport, CT: Greenwood Press.

Daniels, H., & Bizar, M. (1998). *Methods that matter.* York, Maine: Stenhouse Publishers.

Daniels, H., & Zemelman, S. (2004). *Subjects matter: Every teacher's guide to content-area reading.* Portsmouth, NH: Heinemann.

Davidson, J., & Lytle, M. (2000). *After the fact: The art of historical detection.* Boston: McGraw Hill.

Degelman, C., & Hayes, B. (1995). *Active citizenship today field guide.* Los Angeles, CA: Constitutional Rights Foundation.

Donovan, M. S. & Bransford, J. D., eds. (2005). *How students learn: History in the classroom.* Washington, DC: National Academies Press.

Doty, J. K., Cameron, G. N., & Barton, M. L. (2003). *Teaching reading in social studies: A supplement to teaching reading in the content areas.* Alexandria, VA: Association for Supervision and Curriculum Development.

Drake, F., & Nelson, L. (2005). *Engagement in teaching history: Theory and practices for middle and secondary teachers.* Upper Saddle River, NJ: Pearson Education, Inc.

Furay, C., & Salevouris, M. J. (2002). *The methods and skills of history: A practical guide.* Wheeling, IL: Harlan Davidson, Inc.

Gaddy, B. B., Marzano, R. J., Paynter, D. E., & Pickering, D. J. (2004). *Handbook for classroom instruction that works.* New York, NY: Prentice Hall.

Gerwin, D., & Zevin, J. (2003). *Teaching U.S. history as mystery.* Portsmouth, NH: Heinemann.

Grinder, M. (1995). *ENVoY: A personal guide to classroom management.* Battle Ground, WA: Michael Grinder and Associates.

Harris, J. (1998). *Design tools for the Internet-supported classroom.* Alexandria, VA: Association for Supervision and Curriculum Development.

Heidrich, D. (1999). *Relevant reading: Investigating historical documents in today's world.* Michigan: Instructional Fair.

International Center for Leadership in Education (2002). *Rigor and relevance handbook.* New York, NY: International Center for Leadership in Education.

Keene, E. O., & Zimmermann, S. (1997). *Mosaic of thought: Teaching comprehension in a reader's workshop.* Portsmouth, NH: Heinemann.

Kelnor, L. (1993). *The creative classroom: A guide for using creative drama in the classroom.* Portsmouth, NH: Heinemann.

Kuhn, C., & McLellan, M. L. (1997). Oral history. *OAH Magazine of History.* (Spring).

Macceca, S. (2007). *Reading Strategies for Social Studies.* Huntington Beach, CA: Shell Education.

Partin, R. L. (1995). *Classroom teacher's survival guide: Practical strategies, management techniques, and reproducibles for new and experienced teachers.* New York, NY: Center for Applied Research in Education.

Pelisson, G. (2003). *Mastering social studies skills.* New York, NY: Amsco Publications.

Percoco, J. (1998). *A Passion for the Past: Creative teaching in U.S. history.* Portsmouth NH: Heinemann.

Popham, W. J. (2001). *The truth about testing: An educator's call to action.* Alexandria, VA: Association for Supervision and Curriculum Development.

Quigley, C., Fischer, M., Rodriguez, K., & Bahmueller, C. (2007). *Project citizen.* Calabasas, CA: Center for Civic Education.

Reading Quest.org. Making sense in social studies. http://www.readingquest.org.

Robb, L. (2004). *Nonfiction writing from the inside out.* New York, NY: Scholastic.

Robb, L. (2003). *Teaching reading in social studies, science, and math.* New York, NY: Scholastic.

Roberts, R., & Olson, J. S. (1994). *American experiences: Readings in American history.* New York: Harper Collins.

Ruddell, M. R. (2005). *Teaching content reading and writing*. NJ: John Wiley and Sons.

Silver, H. F., Strong, W., Perini, M., & Reilly, E. (2001). *The interactive lecture: Research-based strategies for teachers*. Woodbridge, NJ: The Thoughtful Education Press.

Social Education Magazine by NCSS provides yearly "Best Books in Social Studies."

Sommer, B. W., & Quinlan, M. K. (2002). *The oral history manual*. Walnut Creek, CA: AltaMira Press.

Stiggins, R. (1994). *Assessing reasoning in the classroom*. Portland, OR: Assessment Training Institute, Inc.

Tompkins, G. (2007). *Teaching vocabulary: 50 creative strategies, grades 6-12*. Upper Saddle River, NJ: Prentice Hall.

Vest, K. (2005). *Using primary sources in the classroom*. Huntington Beach, CA: Shell Education.

Wineburg. S. (2001). *Historical thinking and other unnatural acts: Charting the future of teaching the past*. Philadelphia, PA: Temple University Press.

Wolf, P. (2001) *Brain Matters*. Alexandria, VA: Association for Supervision and Curriculum Development.